FISHING
WIDOWS

By the same author

JONES VERY: SELECTED POEMS (*editor*)

THE SEASONABLE ANGLER

FISHERMAN'S BOUNTY (*editor*)

FISHING WIDOWS

BY NICK LYONS

CROWN PUBLISHERS, INC.
New York

For Mari, always

I am grateful to Herb Michelman, Pat Winsor, Jean Crawford, and Jerry Hoffnagle for valuable suggestions, and to the following magazines for permission to reprint material which originally appeared in their pages:

Field & Stream magazine: "Why 50 Million People Fish" and "A Tale of Two Fishes"

Sports Afield magazine: "The Legacy," "Lies from Blue River," "On the Divide (which also appears in *Fishing Moments of Truth,* © by James Rikhoff and Eric Peper, Winchester Press, 1973)

Random Casts: "Night-Fishing" and "The Perils of Fly-Fish-Book Editing"

Trout magazine: "Matching the Catch"

Fly Fisherman magazine: "Trout in Fun City," "The Fine Art of Hudson River Fence Fishing," and "My Secret Life" (under the title "Battenkill Nocturne"). Reprinted from *Fly Fisherman* magazine, Manchester, Vermont 05254.

True Fishing Yearbook: "Big Muddy" (which appeared there in a sharply compacted form)

Contents

Part One

CITY-BOUND
AND THEORIZING

Premises

MY LIFE FOR MANY YEARS HAS BEEN bound by a city. A grey, dry, sunless place—swarming like an anthill with people. It is a world of ''getting and spending,'' of busy offices and crises and gossip, of financial pressure and itching fear—of living, to a great extent, outside of oneself.

Fishing—in the brain and on the rivers—has been my antidote to all this. It is green and generous. If it is not always idyllic, it always gives me back part of myself that has been lost somewhere among the endless papers. I never go to rivers to kill hecatombs of trout or, actually, any trout: I go to unkill parts of myself that otherwise might die.

Fishing is an irrelevant passion. Wars, financial responsibilities, high art, politics, domestic relations—oh, one could name

3

just about anything in the busy city world, or anywhere, and it will have more relevance than fishing.

Fishing is *complexly* irrelevant, and its very capacity to absorb men completely makes it the more valuable to them—and the less intelligible to women. A woman may not like the idea of a mistress, but another woman is something she can understand and fight. Fishing—unintelligible and irrelevant to the uninitiate —is, as the wise judge Robert Traver wisely notes, *worse* than adultery. The very intensity of the passion—often private, occasionally even religious—is of course what creates fishing widows, and I doubt if the strange predicament of the women, the frequent chauvinism of the men, can be understood or appreciated without some disclosure of how deeply the fisherman's passion runs.

Mine's unfathomable.

I understand Kafka better.

Not all the stories, reminiscences, and imaginings in this book are about that unique phenomenon the fishing widow. Some are about the fish-madness itself, which causes all the mischief; some are about rivers, which are often so feminine in their enticements; and some are about the absence of rivers in one's life, which makes the angler's heart grow fonder.

Some fishing widows suffer loudly, some silently. I have known some who learned to live royally on their husbands' guilt. Some women won't be made fishing widows and make fishless widows of their husbands. Some fishing widows are sons—and some sons graduate from that role.

It is an entanglement that may issue both pain and humor— and someday, hopefully, even understanding.

1

The Legacy

I HAD NEVER KNOWN ED HALLIDAY, OF course—neither personally nor by reputation. For a while after that night I tried to find someone who had: someone who had fished with the man, someone who could tell me how he approached a pool, what rivers he loved, how softly he could lay down a dry fly, what size stripers he took from which lonely beaches, whether he preferred flat water or the riffles, whether he fished often, in the early mornings, weekdays, autumns, or when and where and how.

But I was not very successful and to tell the truth I didn't try very hard. After that evening I had my own image of the man and whatever he actually was has by now been transformed in my imagination. I have never even seen a photograph of him. Once I was tempted to ask Tom for one, but I never did. Not even after he finally saw his father. After all, his legacy was not mine.

My former student Tom Halliday had called late one night to ask my advice. His father had died a few months earlier and there was, he said, a certain amount of fishing equipment in the estate. Would I come over and give him an educated opinion?

"Doesn't anyone in the family fish?" I asked. I was rather too busy that wet December to go tramping the bleak cold city looking at some poor dead bloke's cod rods. I hadn't mentioned fishing for three months and my marriage was flourishing. I knew Tom had never cast a line, for I now and then make allusions to trouting in my classes: there are metaphors in it for most of what goes on in the world. He had never risen, except once, to ask a sharp and probing question about the "morality" of trout fishing. I had rather worked my way out of the trout-killing business, and he said it was worse to play with them and then throw them back; he could understand a man fishing for food.

Tom had never mentioned his father to me, though the number of times he came to me for certain advice might have suggested that he had no father to ask—or that, as for so many young people today, the bridge had been blown up. I knew he was searching for values, for a guide; he was not by nature a rebel and his solitary nature kept him from joining the fashionable student mobs. We shared certain solitary habits of mind.

No. None of the family fished: neither of his two sisters, certainly not his mother, none of his uncles. And they didn't want to bring in a dealer until they had some idea how much the lot was worth. The man had fished a great deal, Tom told me, and his sisters thought the equipment might have substantial value.

"Are any of the rods in metal cases?" I asked. "Tubes?"

Tom did not remember. He only knew there was now a mass of it in several closets where his sisters lived and that he had been given a quick look a few weeks after the funeral.

"Didn't you see it in the house?" I asked. "When your father was alive?"

"I didn't live with my father. My parents were divorced. I was only allowed to see him three, maybe four times."

I agreed to take a quick look and, to the best of my limited ability with such matters, let him know if I thought the tackle had much value. The next evening I met him in the lobby of a dowdy apartment building on the upper West Side.

The apartment was a shambles. Beer cans were littered everywhere; clothes and newspapers were carelessly heaped in the corners; I thought I detected the odor of marijuana. The television was blasting from the other end of the living room and the lights were dimmed. A seductive but sleazy girl in her mid-twenties was scrunched down into the shoulder of the couch and, as we came in, a bearded young man moved over to the opposite arm lazily, frowned, and then stared back at the set.

Tom said the girl was Clarise, his older sister; he'd never seen this particular friend of hers. He brought me directly into a large cluttered room and told me to wait a moment while he fetched his younger sister, Julie. I pivoted slowly in the dim room, trying to find some logic to this bewildering mess.

I could not.

A few moments later a whole spate of fishing rods, clustered and extended like lances, came thrusting into the room. There were eight or nine of them together, with one long stick projecting ahead of the others. Even before I saw who was carrying them, I saw the long rod catch against a cardboard crate and bend suddenly in a sharp arc. I leaped for it, shouted wildly, and managed to shove the crate back. I was too late.

"Damn," I muttered. "Clean split."

The girl—quite short, scraggly, and obviously very hip—was unruffled. "Did something drop?" she asked.

"No," I said after a short pause.

"What was that sound? Like didn't you hear something, Tommy?"

"You broke one of the rods," I said. I still couldn't see, among the mess of sticks, which one had snapped. Most of them were thick saltwater affairs.

"I couldn't have!" she announced.

I turned the light on, went over to the pile of rods she'd summarily dropped on the daybed, and showed her the split tip section. I shut my eyes. It was a fine light-ocher bamboo.

The girl looked at it closely, running her fingers across the severed strands. Then she proclaimed, in the miraculous tone of admitting something she rarely admitted: "Like you're right!"

Tom had come over, and he, too, wanted to see the rod.

I disengaged it carefully from the others and held it out, the splintered tip hanging limply where it had broken. It was a fly rod—about eight feet, I judged—and a fine one. I grasped the cork handle instinctively, thumb ahead. Fine fly rods come alive in your hand: this one leaped, then died. I could feel it in my stomach.

Then my eyes darted to the butt.

The signature read:

Dickerson   *7604*
         Ed Halliday

"No. No. No."

"Is it a good one?" asked Tom.

"One of the best," I muttered. "Custom-made, too. Is there another tip for this?"

The girl said she'd look and skipped out of the room.

Tom could see that I was upset and asked if the rod could be fixed. I told him it couldn't, not anymore, but that a company on the coast could probably match the broken section from their stock, or build another. It would be expensive, and the rod would probably never be quite the same.

"I don't like to see fine things destroyed," Tom said soberly. "I don't know a Dickerson from a Weyerhaeuser, but if you say it's one of the best . . ."

"It should have been in a metal case. I can't imagine why it was set up like that," I said, bending the splintered tip gently so that the pieces came together—imperfectly.

"Julie!" called Tom. "Have you found a case for this rod? Or another . . . another . . .?"

"Tip," I said quietly. "Tip section."

"Another tip?"

She came into the room with a heaping armful of tackle, cases, and boxes, dumped them onto the daybed, and went back for more. "No cases yet. But I think I saw some near the radiator."

I shuddered visibly and Tom asked me if I wanted a drink.

"Two."

"Let's go into the kitchen."

Several quick shots of Jack Daniels didn't help. And I was anxious and troubled about returning to the room. When we got back the pile had grown substantially. Julie was bringing in, she said, the last of it. She did. She dropped a couple of fly boxes, a handful of empty reel cases, and a net upon the rest, sighed, and said: "I never realized Ed had so much junk. Clarise brought some over the day we closed up his place, and I took some over in a duffel bag on Harvey's bike, and the uncles carried some. I never saw it all together like this before. There's a regular mountain of it, this junk, isn't there, Tommy?"

Though the equipment was in wild disarray, and most of it buried, it was simple enough to see that it had substantial value. There were seven or eight Wheatley fly boxes, six or seven aluminum rod tubes in canvas or leather carrying cases, a fisherman's carryall, a fine pair of Hodgman waders, a lovely English wicker creel, seven or eight expensive saltwater reels to go with the heavy rods I'd seen. And more.

Much more.

It was also simple enough to see that though the equipment was heaped and disordered now, the man himself had been meticulous. One quick look into the opened top of a Wheatley fly box disclosed that. Here and there were corners of his fishing life untouched by his pelican daughters.

I held out my arms, smiled, and said, with as little irony as possible: "How can I help?"

Tom explained that the provisions of their father's will had simply said that all his worldly possessions were to become, jointly, the property of Julie, Clarise, and himself. His mother, Rena, had gotten some cash and, when it was secured, had gone off on one of her frequent trips—this time, one of the girls thought, to South America. But they weren't sure.

They had decided to sell all this "fishing junk" and divide the proceeds equally—if indeed it had any value; but Tom could have his choice of several items if he had any use for them; the girls certainly didn't. They had heard hostile talk about fishing from their mother for as long as they could remember. "I suppose what we'd like is some evaluation of it all," said Tom, "and perhaps some help for me in choosing one outfit. I didn't want any of it at first, but there's something fascinating about it, isn't there? I doubt that I'll ever use any of it, but I guess that since these things obviously meant something to him, I should keep some of it."

"All right," I said, "let's unravel the debris."

I began by extracting the saltwater equipment. The big rods were good fiber glass; I suggested their commonness and minimal resale value. Some of the big-game reels looked expensive and I mentioned several places that dealt in such used equipment; I told the confused legatees to try them all, and to take the best offer.

In a half hour we had gone through all of the heavy gear— surf-casting rods and spinning reels, boat rods and reels, carryalls full of hooks and lures and wire leaders. It all probably had cost in excess of a thousand dollars, but I told them to be satisfied with several hundred. Through private sales they might get more; but they would have to advertise, and without someone knowledgeable on hand, it would be a cumbersome business.

The freshwater tackle was another matter.

Nothing here was cheap; nothing was less than choice. The gear was all for trout, and it was the best. I could not quite reconcile it with the heavy saltwater tackle, but that was my fault: the world of trout has seemed mysterious enough to me since I found it, perhaps for a lifetime.

I said nothing for a long time while I carefully laid out the fly rods, cases, boxes, and miscellaneous gear, each separately and in a safe section of the room. Several times I thought I detected Tom's eyes searching mine while I fingered a particularly fine item.

None of the rods were in their cases. One other besides the Dickerson was fully joined, and I began with these first, trying to match up odd tips with mid and butt sections, some of them warped from heat, nicked badly, and otherwise damaged.

"Why weren't these in their cases?" I asked without looking up, as I laid out the three sections of a handsome eight-and-a-half-foot Wes Jordan Orvis.

"We—ll," said Julie. "Like Harvey was over and he wanted to see it all . . ."

"Does Harvey fish?"

"Only from the piers at Sheepshead Bay now and then. He drives this motorcycle, see, and he likes to go down there and sit on the piers and drink a few beers on a hot summer evening."

"Why didn't he put them back?"

"Well, a couple of weeks ago we had it all out, every stitch of it, you see, and well, we were having a little fun with the rods and then it seemed like one helluva lot of trouble to . . ."

"Fun?"

"Some of us were . . . a little high, and we were like fencing with the really thin jobbies."

"Like this one?" I asked her, holding up the extra tip to the Dickerson. It had several bad nicks in its finish and one guide had been ripped off, but it looked straight and solid still.

"Guess that's one of them."

"And what's this piece of heavy wool doing on the end of this one?" My God, the fully joined rod was a Payne, seven-and-a-half-foot.

"The cat."

Tom had grown strawberry red. "What about the cat?"

"We were fishing for it."

I closed my eyes and rubbed my forehead. Then I disjointed the rod, running my fingers along its smooth redbrown surface. With old Jim Payne gone, his fine rods had recently trippled in value; in ten years they would be priceless.

There were no reels to be found for any of the fly rods: no one knew what had happened to them. And there was one case for which we could find no rod. It had been an Orvis midge. Julie finally admitted she had given it to Harvey.

"The motorcyclist? The guy who fishes off piers?" My voice was high and shrill.

"Look, mister, don't talk that way about him. I can do what I want with Ed's possessions. What did he ever do for me? Clarise knows and she couldn't care less. Who are you to come in here making snide remarks? This is my apartment and my junk and I can do exactly what I want with it."

"Shut up, will you!" said Tom abruptly. "I invited him here to help us. The rod you gave away may have been worth a few hundred dollars. And it was Dad's."

"Well, it's not Ed's anymore. I don't care if it was worth ten thousand bucks. Like it was Harvey's birthday and I told him to pick out a couple of things. He liked that skinny little stick and I'm glad he's got it."

"Look, Tom. Maybe I'd better go. This is family business. This equipment was obviously the man's life. It's the very best, and since I take it he wasn't very rich he probably bought it with every spare nickel he had, out of the deepest kind of passion and love. It has financial value. A lot. The demand for a number of these rods—the Dickerson, the Payne, that Garrison—will continue to increase, like blue chips. Make the lot of it neat, get a dealer in, or a couple of them, and get bona fide appraisals. I'll leave you some names. Maybe it will end up in someone's hands who will appreciate what's here."

I straightened my jacket and asked where my coat was.

"Stay a little longer," said Tom. "Julie, shut your mouth for ten minutes, will you?"

The girl balled up her fist and, shaking her head, walked slowly out of the room.

When she was gone I took two or three quick, deep breaths.

"It's a disaster, isn't it?" said Tom.

"It's criminal," I said quietly. "Look at these fly boxes: they've been left on a radiator—they're all rusted and most of the flies are ruined. See this flytying equipment? The man probably tied each one of those several thousand flies himself. It's meticulous work. Look closely at this Hendrickson. See how carefully it's made? See how straight the tail comes off the shank of the hook? The neat uprightness of the mandarin wings? The delicate pink in the body? The neatly tapered head knot?"

I held the fly out and Tom took it. He held it lightly at the barb and brought it close and then back a few inches from his face. He nodded his head and handed it back to me.

"And look at these feathers scattered across the floor," I said. "Ripped out of the necks. Look. Blue dun hackle—excellent grade; you can't buy blue dun necks like this today. Mashed. Ruined. The net's broken, but you could bind up the wood carefully with bait-casting line and varnish it; you can't buy another old miniature net like this anymore: it's a beautiful little thing and probably helped the man with hundreds of memorable trout. Broken rods, missing reels, fishing for cats with a Payne! My God, Tom, whether you fish or not, it's absolutely criminal to treat fine equipment like this; it's like trampling on someone's white linen with muddy feet."

Clarise came in then, let her shoulders slump a full five inches, put a strand of hair in her mouth, and mumbled, "Oh, goddamn: this will take months to clean." Then she said: "Look, Tommy, there are a couple of dozen legal matters I gotta talk over with you and Julie since Rena's skipped, and she wants to get out and meet Harvey. So if you can spare ten minutes from all this heady junk, maybe we can get them done. Already it's time to be finished with this lousy cheap stuff—or are you falling in love with it, like Ed did?"

Tom agreed to go in and asked if I'd mind staying alone for fifteen minutes.

"Not at all," I said. "I'd like to look at all this . . . tackle carefully."

"Be back soon," he said and walked out the doorway. Clarise went after him, took his arm, and whispered loudly: "Can we trust him?"

"No," said Tom in full voice.

I picked up a couple of the rods and waved them back and forth, perpendicular to my waist. I popped open a few more fly boxes. *Perhaps,* I thought, *I should make a low offer for it all and try to steal the whole lot. In a week they'll mash it all anyway. It will be worthless. Cats!*

I picked up the vest, carried it over to an armchair, sat down wearily, and began going through the pockets. My wife would be wondering where I was; I had enough trouble breaking away for a few hours' fishing: I didn't much want this disaster to keep me out half the night, in December, when my most family instincts usually emerged.

But the vest was fascinating.

Leader material. Spare leaders, dyed bluebrown. Penknife, small and sharp. Fly dope. Leader sink. Rubber leader-straightening pad. Matted pack of matches.

I put my hand into an inside pocket. *What's this?* I fished out a little black notebook.

I thumbed through it slowly and saw that it was a record of trips, in a neat fine hand. There was a date, the abbreviation of several streams I had fished, a few scattered comments about the condition of the water, an emergence record, and finally, for each day, a list of trout caught and the fly that had taken them.

He had done well.

It was a pleasant, valuable little book—with a wealth of stream information of the kind that would fascinate any hard-core addict like myself. I would have liked to study it carefully, and half thought of taking it. Who would miss it? Who, among his children, would understand it?

Toward the end of the book he had written something else; it took the last six or seven pages. I cannot remember it all, but some words riveted themselves to my brain.

Raining. Sheets and sweeps of it. River growing browner by the minute. River pocked with bubbles and the lines slanting in. So I sit under this ledge, with pipe and pen, with my good Dickerson taken down and lying across my knees. Gulleys of brown water washing down around me. But it's dry here, and there are two nice trout in my basket and I released four more this morning, which started so quietly before sunup, alone, with the mists hovering over the river. Rena would never understand. Never did. Not Clarise. Not Julie. Not ever. Not even the shrill crisp of the morning or the quick disappearance of a dry fly. Not the swallows sweeping down the stream's alley, the stream birds beginning to work when a good hatch gets under way. Not the deep satisfaction of laying down a good cast, several in a row, sixty or seventy feet of line poised in the air and then reaching toward the eddy behind the midstream rock. Not the squirrel who shared my snack a half hour ago. Not the colors of the water or the sharp, sudden tug of a fat native trout. They never did. They never will. I was never able to tell them the slightest small bit of it, not any of them.

And Tom I do not know.

One calls it butchery while she butchers everything private and holy in her and everyone near her; another finds it merely boring. Fine. Each to his own.

Rena tells me I want to be a little boy again.

And Tom, they have never let me know.

Good ladies, I find myself here. The confusions disappear. The sweet mystery of it envelops me. It is full of sweet noises, the air. Perhaps I have failed with you all. You certainly have failed me and perhaps yourselves.

And Tom? I wish to God you could have been here this morning, my son. Whispering while we suited up in the dark before dawn, talking about flies and stream conditions, and a certain, particular trout one or the other of us raised six weeks earlier. He is the one person I would truly have loved to fish with, to communicate the loveliness of being alone with the streams and the trees and the mysteries under the surface. He is the one person I should have liked to tell this morning to, rain and all. Mud and all. Tom, you are my only son and I can give you nothing. You will not call now, now that you are a man. You *cannot* call, you cannot speak to me. I cannot even hope that someday, somehow, you will find me, or this piece of bamboo, or this corner of the world where a man can still husband that sure and gentle legacy that is every man's . . .

I closed the little black book and waved it back and forth vigorously. Then I rose, still holding it, and began to walk swiftly to the door.

I heard voices coming toward me. I picked up the vest, slipped the book into its hiding place, and dropped it casually on the heap.

"Well, I've seen it all, Tom, and there's nothing much more I can say. This trout equipment is valuable. The Payne, even though it's been used for cat fishing, is probably worth four hundred dollars or more; the Dickerson somewhat less; the flies can't be sold; the net and boots, this and that, have no resale value."

"What would you suggest?"

I hesitated. "I know you don't fish . . ."

"I think I'd like to try, perhaps this spring."

"It could be arranged."

"I might have to reimburse my sisters if I took it all. Should I?"

"That's your affair, Tom. But there's something of a man you never knew, who you've wanted to know, I think, in all this."

"Perhaps," he said, looking away from me.

Neither of us spoke for a moment.

"Well, take the Dickerson," I said, "and, if you can get it, the Payne. But if you fish, don't use them for a full couple of years. Learn on a good glass rod and use it until . . . well, until it seems to be part of your arm. I can show you a little about it this spring if you're really interested. Buy an inexpensive reel for the glass rod, and then, when you're ready, the best reel you can afford—a Hardy or an Orvis. The flies might still be good. Some of them. Go through them carefully some night when you have a few hours. But put away one of each pattern, in cork, for a reminder. The waders are ruined. Keep the net."

"Anything else?"

"No," I said. "I guess that's all."

"I'm grateful to you," he said, extending his hand.

I reached out to him, but drew my hand back. "Oh, yes," I said. "Take the vest." I picked it up and handed it to him. "It has no value," I said quietly. "No value whatsoever. But there are a few items in it that will show you what a proper vest should contain. Your father wore if often, I think, and perhaps you'll find something in it that will help you understand who he was. Otherwise, it has no value."

2

Why Fifty Million People Fish

THERE IS A CURIOUS RUMOR THAT FISH-
ing is idyllic and pastoral, that it rejuvenates
the spirit and excites the blood to high adven-
ture, that it requires high intelligence. Here
in the city I often dream of idyllic days, when mayflies, tan against
a sinking sun, crowd off the water, flutter in clouds down the alley
of a stream, and the fish make the surface pocked and choppy with
their feeding.

But then I remember: my experience has been otherwise.

Your boat leaks. It rains. You fall in, freeze, boil, hook yourself, hook your partner, lose your equipment, catch the weeds,
catch pneumonia, snarl your line, get bitten by flies you can't
see, miss the big one, and hear, inevitably, that you should have
been there yesterday or last week or next month. If you return alive
and sane, no one believes a word you tell them; if you stay out too

17

long or too often, you lose your family or your job. If you don't stay out long enough, he who did will taunt you unto death that "they began to bite like mad ten minutes after you left."

You don't want to neglect your wife, so you take her along: she gets bitten to shreds by black flies and doesn't speak to you for a year. You take your children along, since you've heard in these hard times the family that fishes together stays together: you spend the day untying knots, the kiddies fall in, you bring them home sopping wet and sneezing, and your wife doesn't speak to you for a year.

You drive three hundred miles for striped bass fishing: there's a hurricane.

You fly to Montana in June: there's a snowstorm.

You get up at two in the morning and collapse before you get to your favorite stream. You *get* to your favorite stream—but nine million guys have gotten there before you. I once knew a man who swore he'd caught a one-pound bass. But he was a heavy drinker.

They say that man has evolved. Fishing disproves it.

In 1496, when Wynken de Worde published Dame Juliana Berners's *A Treatys of Fyshing with an Angle*, it was possible to fish a whole year for respectable fish with a few cents' worth of equipment; in the Stone Age it was cheaper, and the fish were larger. Today more than three billion dollars is spent annually by those called in the national surveys "habitual anglers."

And the fish are smaller and fewer and no smarter.

On certain salmon rivers, the average fisherman spends more than three hundred dollars per salmon caught; it's cheaper to have a dozen air-shipped from Scotland, and you don't have to worry about the black flies.

President Grover Cleveland, who this once knew whereof he spoke, pronounced: "At the outset, the fact should be recognized that the community of fishermen constitute a class or subrace among the inhabitants of the earth." Subrace. There's a message in that word. And in the word "habitual," too. "Good luck" is the traditional greeting among brothers of the angle. I propose "Good grief!"

I have been fishing since before I can remember, which is

longer than I've been doing anything that I can remember, so I
might be considered an authority on why fifty million people fish.
I've also researched the issue as closely as I dare: the results are
frightening. One psychologist claims it is behavioral conditioning;
another speaks of it as a "submergence syndrome," a return to
the mother sea; others say there is covert hostility in all fishermen.
Not against the fish, I'm sure: against oneself. No matter. It is
the great humbler of man. No one understands why people fish.
The mystery, as Poe would say, will not be understood.

Still, there are some facts.

Consider how rational men in the twentieth century pursue
three billion dollars' worth of what they could buy for a couple of
dollars in their local fish markets.

On April Fools', whether it falls on the first of the month or
the last Saturday, thousands of otherwise sane and responsible
men rise long before sunup, drive through dark city streets, along
bleak deserted highways to their idyllic stream, and then ritual-
istically immerse themselves in icy water. The temperature is
below freezing, ice forms at the guides of their rods, they think
desperately of excuses to wives and children at home (who imagine
this is *fun?*) and by noon—unless they have been in rigorous train-
ing for this ordeal—they are insensate, barely able to stand.

I know. I've been there.

The next day the newspapers carry photos of strange figures
from a subrace of man, and a bewildering tangle of poles and
lines. Some are wearing Arctic gear, others crouch around a
streamside fire like cavemen; it could be Siberia or the steppes.
But if you look closely you will always see one beaming face, and
hanging by the jaws from a stick several small reasons for the glee.

Fortunately, for many of these men the season will be over in
a month, and then they will go out no more, but turn to golf or coun-
try-club tennis, to wives or badminton, or to any of a hundred more
socially acceptable and comfortable ways of spending their leisure
moments.

But many remain in the brotherhood of the angle. Some spend
thousands of dollars, days on end in the scorching sun, pursuing
saltwater sea monsters it will take them hours to land; others stand

on party boats, thirty abreast, having a party hauling up cod. If you think cod fishing's fun, try attaching a clothesline to a can of garbage and lifting it five stories in the wind.

Worst, by far, are the trout fishermen.

And most long-suffering, by far, are the trout fishing widows.

A guy named Art Flick once spent three years doing nothing but catching and identifying the bugs trout eat. He carried a rod only so other fishermen wouldn't think he was nuts. Maybe those were the best years of his life. Trout fishermen are the subrace within the subrace.

Which is pretty low.

Trout fishermen spend endless hours tying bits of bird's feathers onto tiny wire hooks. They have been known to slip into a mystical trance at the mere mention of the holy names "Big Hole," "Firehole," "Neversink," "Snake." They learn enough Latin to mumble about *Iron fraudators* and *Ephemerella subvarias* and *Stenonema fuscums*. They attend panel discussions and slide presentations by experts and learned entomologists, which prolong the fishing-widow season to all seasons. They study esoteric books like *Matching the Hatch* and *A Modern Dry-Fly Code*. They collect sticks of bamboo worth three and four hundred dollars. And all for what? For a creature that averages about the weight of two Idaho potatoes and has a brain smaller than a chick-pea.

Evolution?

Why do more than fifty million people *really* fish? Maybe only one man knows. Twenty-five years ago that sage, Mr. Edward Zern, claimed that "roughly two-thirds of all fishermen never eat fish. This should surprise nobody. Fish is brain food. People who eat fish have large, well-developed brains. People with large, well-developed brains don't fish."

But he was only half right. There were less than twenty-five million fishermen then.

3
Matching the Catch

THE ASTUTE ERNEST SCHWIEBERT HAS long since been recognized for his mastery of the ultimate technique of "matching the hatch." It is said that not only do trout take his feathered imitations eagerly but that naturals mate with his matches. Let the scoffers scoff about the possibility of such; when they are Mr. Schwiebert's masters, they will catch what he catches.

But catching is not killing, and there is an even deadlier principle of trout fishing, one that no doubt accounts for larger kills. It is not restricted to trout. It scores for hackleheads, ling, whiting, and cod. Its power lies less in the realm of exact science than in the psychology of subliminal pull. There is really no better name for it, and I want to go on record, and be accorded the distinction in some McDonald's history of these angling times, as naming it "matching the catch."

A good deal has been said about the effect of wives, children, mothers-in-law, and other fishing widows as direct and pernicious influences on the number of fish killed. There is much truth in this. The credibility gap is nowhere less bridgeable than between the purist with barbless hooks and his Philistine relatives who, lacking all regard for the sport and trust for the truth, demand that fish caught be verified by fish in the sink. I have seen good men succumb to such pressure and, out of a nice and unnecessary respect for their marriages, become arrant killers.

A good deal has also been said about those magazines that flourish by displaying the fruits of fishing in bright dead color on their pages. A picture is no doubt worth a thousand wrong words, and these are no doubt proof positive and indisputable that this or that expert indeed is expert; but I modestly propose that at least one magazine, once, display a four-color photograph of a man in obvious bliss, in holy beatitude, holding open an empty creel.

A man can, or should be able to, resist the sarcasm of his wife, his children, and his mother-in-law. He should indeed have enough will to withstand the suggestiveness of photographs—for have we not all been insulated by the advertisers? But who can withstand the pressure of a friend catching and creeling fish after fish a hundred yards upstream—especially when there are other friends waiting back at the camp?

I first observed this principle during the years when I was a sad victim of the Opening Day Madness—for which a three-week cold and a near-collapse from exhaustion were the ideal and poetic cure. We would stand in a line, four of us, and haul them in—the faster the better. We had not heard about throwing them back. It was not in our vocabulary. A fish caught by a friend was a threat; two caught made the others frantic; one of us sitting by a tree, limited-out, put the others into a state of acute anxiety neurosis.

Later, I was amazed to observe the same principle among sophisticated fly-fishermen. One man can ruin twenty in this respect for, as Prince Hamlet—that fisher after truth—observed: "One dram of eal, the noble substance" corrupts. Good men, quite content, alone, to have caught and released a dozen trout, will turn killers upon observing a friend with several big dead trout in the creel—all handsome and bright in their fern and grassy coffins. I knew one who the very next morning rose at four, fished intensely for six hours, and appeared nonchalantly with three dead trout a trifle larger than those caught and killed the day before. A little later, another good man kept five; then one kept six.

Better to bring a few home to your wife now and then, to encourage her to believe you do *not* have a mistress but are indeed trout fishing, than to lapse into such barbaric competition.

I know of one pair of families from Virginia who make a holy pilgrimage to the Beaverkill every June for two weeks. They leave with shopping bags full of frozen trout. I have spoken with each of the men privately, and alone each seems sensible. Together they make it a two-horse race, winner take nothing. It is bad enough to find Barnhart's Pool turned into a coliseum; it is tragic to fight it out tooth and claw with your best friend for high hook. "Men think in herds," says Charles MacKay, "but they recover their senses slowly, and one by one."

As for all diseases there is a cure, I should like to make the following modest proposals—though, since they are sensible, I cannot think they will be accepted. I would suggest:

(1) divorce;
(2) a year's moratorium on photos of dead trout;
(3) a year's moratorium on fishing with even one other person;
(4) a two-week full-time job in a fresh-fish shop;
(5) writing six thousand times Father Walton's maxim that fishing is a virtue in itself.

And then, perhaps, we can not only match the hatch—as Mr. Schwiebert and others have in their wisdom taught us to do—but hatch the catch, by returning it. And when we have done this, we can fish together again without scorecards, photograph and keep a trout or two perhaps, and even notice that the birches are changing color.

We might even remember that, alas, our wives must learn to trust us not for the trout we catch but for ourselves.

But I do not believe it will take place in my lifetime.

4

Lies from Blue River

I NOW HAVE UNDENIABLE PROOF THAT either Horace or Sam is an outright liar.

Don't think I haven't suspected it! But trust is as much a part of the angler's anatomy as mendacity, and I've given these "good friends" the benefit of my trust for years. What a fool I've been. Here in the city, fishing vicariously through their letters, I've been made the biggest red sucker in the pool.

Judge for yourself. This morning I received, in the same mail, their "expert" reports from Blue River, which, the way they talk, you'd think they own.

Horace's letter, in part, said: "The Blue is definitely off—horrible these past weeks. No surface action whatsoever. None. No fish working. Never had such a season. Never."

Sam's read: "I simply could not have had better fishing this week on my old Blue River. Water conditions perfect. Great fly life coming off. Took a sixteen-incher on the top Monday during a spectacular hatch, and picked up half a dozen more yesterday morning. *And last night?* Don't ask!''

I am a patient man but I fish too little and dream too much. I look lovingly at puddles here in the great city. I investigate rumors that eels are being taken through the manholes on First Avenue. On a particularly bad week, I walk twenty blocks out of my way to watch rainbow trout in the window tanks of Allen's Restaurant.

You think that's funny?

It's hell.

And how do you think I feel when those "friends" lie to me in their teeth when I'm in such a mood? And I'm in one now. So help me.

Here I've gone and wasted a whole afternoon of work brooding over those letters. I didn't get to Abercrombie's to check out their new Payne. Nothing. The possibilities are maddening. Horace, despite those consistently lucky days he has when we're on the water together, may well be such a miserable fisherman he couldn't catch chub in a bathtub. It's also possible he's lying so I won't come up this weekend and catch all his lousy trout. And I suppose I can't discount the chance that the Blue's in very poor shape and isn't worth the four-hour trip. He could, this once, be telling it like it is.

But what if he isn't?

What if they're having one of those unbelievable seasons when everything goes right? What if *Sam's* telling the truth for the first time in his life and not cooking up sixteen-inch illusions? Doesn't that make me one hell of a doubting fool? And frankly, this is no time to be made a fool of—not in my condition.

I've always noted a perverse streak in Sam, of course. Like the time he finally took me to that Wallop's Pool he's been whispering about for two years. If that was *really* Wallop's Pool, I'll burn my Orvis. He knew I'd never ask again. Not after *that* trek, in *that* heat, to *that* pool? Which he said we caught on a bad day. But did that stop him? He's discovered four new pools already— all hush-hush, sneaky-peaky.

Of course the man has caught his fish. I've seen them. Though I'll swear one was still cold in the head—and it was 93° that day.

Lying would be nothing new for Horace. He may be my best friend, but in all honesty his fish grow after they're gutted. Those he catches. If he catches any.

Help me! How can a decent man keep his sanity? Gentle sport? Sweet companionship among brothers of the angle? With liars like those two? Connivers? Did you notice how Horace repeated the words "no" and "never"?

Very suspicious.

And the way Sam had to sentimentalize that old muddy ditch of his—which *I* call the Brown? I'm better off fishing for eels on First Avenue, or watching the trout rising in that well-stocked tank at Allen's. My wife never knows, and what she don't know . . .

Will I hit the Blue this weekend? Don't ask!

5

The Perils of
Fly-Fish-Book
Editing

 LAMAR UNDERWOOD, WHO WRITES AN "Adventures in Editing" column for *Sports Afield* is either a Pollyanna or a damned liar. The business of mixing the pleasures of the heart with one's profession isn't an *adventure*: it's a disaster.

Four years ago, I was a sober editor, content to work on a Mosconi billiards book, histories of Greece and the American Revolution and Eastern Europe, pleasantly excited by the smell of a bestseller. Today I'm nearly insane.

Oh, I was a fanatic even then, who kept fly-tying tools on his desk and Flick and Marinaro and Schwiebert under brown paper where reference books should have been. Even then I'd rather fish than eat, and too often preferred fishing to sleep—and even its ancillary pleasures. I'd certainly rather fish than read a book about fishing, and didn't think myself unusual in this: fly-fishing is the sweetest of addictions, I always thought, and most addicts would claim the same. Certainly about books.

But time spent on the river stands in no proportion to that off. None of us—except Al McClane, Frank Woolner, and a half dozen others of the Elect—ever seems to fish enough. So we tie flies, putter with our tackle, meet with fishing friends and conservation clubs, trouble tackle dealers with our interminable love of gab, and drool over the season's Orvis catalog.

Twenty-five years ago, Crown Publishers had bought out the great Derrydale Press one afternoon from Gene Connett and had then generously reverted all the rights back to the authors. They had republished Preston Jennings's *A Book of Trout Flies,* a book of One-Eyed Poacher tales by Edmund Ware Smith, and then an odd fish item or two now and then. All, alas, had been remaindered.

There was a theory among most publishers that the better the angling book the less well it sold; there might be fifty million "habitual" anglers, but they apparently didn't read. Half a dozen of the very best fly-fishing books had been published twenty years ago, and only one or two had earned their keep.

I was not convinced.

My copy of *Art Flick's Streamside Guide* had been destroyed in a devastating fire four years earlier. I combed the tackle shops, but they didn't have it; bookshops thought it might be a picnic manual; even the rare-book dealers hadn't seen a copy in years. So I hunted up Art Flick (who was down south fishing for snook at the time, to keep his arm in practice) and arranged to bring out a new edition. I thought we could sell four or five thousand copies and get an important book back into the hands of guys like me who couldn't tell those damned bugs apart.

It was then I should have realized that disaster was imminent. I was wrong about sales: orders started coming in heavily, long before the book was published. The success was part of my undoing; but I should have realized, from the beginning, something unspeakable was about to happen. "Sorry I can't write much," Art wrote from Jensen Beach, Florida. "Have been fishing for snook and sea trout all day and my wrist is sore."

I consoled him, from my heart: but I didn't see, in his fish-shaking hand, the true handwriting.

With Art's book launched, I went a-looking for others. Vince Marinaro's second letter to me spoke of having a four-pound LeTort brown on for twenty minutes, but losing it because a little weed ball stuck on his leader; I read—and lost that trout with him. Preston Jennings's widow, Adele—a lovely woman—didn't fish: for which I later became enormously grateful.

Now the story gets gruesome.

With the Marinaro and Flick and Jennings out, and all doing extremely well, I began to correspond with dealers and columnists and experts all over the country. "Took a three-pound brown on a dry fly yesterday from the Yellowstone," wrote Dan Bailey in the middle of January.

"Took a thirteen-pound brown in Chile last week," said Ernest Schwiebert, while I chewed pencils and sloshed through city slush.

"The fishing's been so good," wrote Tap Tapply one spring when I had been so busy fly-fish-book editing that I hadn't yet fished, "that I've barely been off the river long enough to sleep."

Mea culpa. Mea maxima culpa.

What had I done to myself?

Doug Swisher returned from, oh, let's call it Leviathan Spring Creek in Montana, and reported taking nearly seventy trout one afternoon on his no-hackles—averaging about sixteen inches.

I was holding two full-time jobs, and doing free-lance work, and trying to see my good wife and four children enough that they wouldn't forget my name, and having these godawful seventy-trout dreams, and surely it was all beginning to unhinge me.

Not to speak of my fishing widow.

When Marinaro calmly told me about a brown trout on his LeTort that ate ducklings for breakfast, it was very nearly too much. I dreamt of that for a month. And I still dream of a Kong of a LeTort brown rising slowly—while Vince calmly snaps an exquisite photo of it for his next slide show—and taking *me*.

Ultimately it was Art Flick who did the gravest damage.

Last May I received this letter. It's typical.

This is a dirty trick to play on you, but do wish you had been along yesterday. There was a big Hendrickson hatch on the Grey and saw seven fish working, no more, no less. Never had such an experience as they were all large fish. No small fish in the lot and they were working in pairs. I managed to get into four, one of which, a big one, got below me and got into a fast run where I couldn't follow; he broke me. Rose another, one of the largest I've ever raised and finally took three, 16¾, 17⅛, 19¼ . . .''

Such precision! The man is *painfully* honest.

I'd finished the letter for the fourth time and had started to congratulate him and say it was all right, I didn't mind being locked in the city, and that I was glad for him, happy with all my heart that he'd had such an afternoon. It wasn't a dirty trick. I didn't care.

But then the afternoon mail was dropped on my desk.

It was a postcard from that rat Flick.

"Lightning struck again today!" I didn't read further.

I wrote him immediately. "What a day I had," I said. "It was drizzling, and last night's rain had formed a beautiful pool on the Left Branch of the East Twenty-ninth, where Park River runs in. The Junction Pool. Looked out of my twentieth-floor window with my telescope and saw seven—*no more, no less*—eels rising. Never had such an experience in my life. They must have come up one of the sewers. Lost one about thirty-two inches on a Grey Fox Variant, and then two—22½ and $23^{17}/_{18}$ inches. Got brought into the Twenty-first Precinct for snarling traffic but the captain was a Fly-for-eels fanatic too. Went back and—would you believe it, Art?—*lightning struck twice!*''

Frankly, I was delighted to be working on *Fishless Days* by Sparse Grey Hackle. He at least claimed not to catch more than two fish in two hundred pages. How deeply one can grow to love that great good-hearted gentleman, with his interminable fund of lore, his magnificent anecdotes, his wit and reverence for the world of angling.

But it was a chimera. It couldn't last.

Sparse might claim not to catch fish but he caught so much more. "A good reporter, that's all," he'd say, and tell me stories that made me laugh and cry, tales of the Mexican Border Patrol and Mr. Hewitt and Ray Bergman and a guy with a Royal Coachman stuck in his nose, and warm recollections of his wife coming off the Junction Pool of the Willowemoc—where George M. L. LaBranche cast the first American dry fly—with an eighteen-inch brown trout.

It became a worse addiction than fishing. We'd talk all afternoon.

So, since it was all piling up, I had to take out my hostility on him. I fixed him up with some speaking engagements, and at one of them he was accosted by a woman with possible designs on him, who called herself Plump Bodied Nymph—which Mr. Miller said was a reasonable description—and we talked about that and other matters piscatorial for a long afternoon, and he got the last couple hundred words on me.

In my sober moments I like to think that fine fly-fishing books are helping, along with groups like Trout Unlimited and the Theodore Gordon Flyfishers, to solidify the American fly-fishing tradition. I like to think that when we are brought together in a common heritage and language, and brought to think deeply about the problems of an art as complex as fly-fishing, we will inevitably take more and more time to *protect* and encourage the sport; that we will respect our quarry and its environment, and respect with our hearts our great rivers and the quality of our pursuit.

But most times this fly-fish-book editing is too heady for my weak constitution.

Lamar can have his "Adventures in Editing." I'll settle for a cane pole, a simple bluegill pond, a couple free hours, and a can of worms.

6

Trout
in Fun City

MY OLD FRIEND CLYDE FISH HAD GOTTEN himself into a bag over mini-rods several months ago, and for the life of me I couldn't see it. He was a meater, a lunker-monger, a man who had always fished for everything from grayling to hackle-heads—any fish at any time, whatever was available. He was not one of those refined chaps who has so much fame and money and distinction that he wants the ultimate distinction of being the only man who, say, caught a Mako shark on a toothpick.

I reminded him of this when we met for our twice-a-week lunch-bag browse on the ninth floor of Abercrombie's. I told him that everything was getting smaller—the world, skirts, the trout, flies, fly rods—and that I simply could not buy it. Except I didn't mind the skirts.

"I need one," he said evasively, hefting a classic eight-foot

Orvis he'd just removed from the rack, "for a very special purpose."

"But you don't believe that nonsense about the whole point of fishing being 'relativity'—fish to tackle size. It's the rivers and the flies, and the sight of a trout rising. You can return as many fish caught on a long rod, can't you? It's as sporting. A person ought to have the best possible rod for the conditions he's fishing . . ."

"Yes!" said Clyde emphatically. "For the conditions."

"Then why waste your money on one of those toothpicks?"

He simply smiled—a benign, condescending smile, I thought.

"Well, whatever the reason," I said, growing furious, "you're contributing to an increasing madness. Why this fishing is getting so canny and persnickety and sporty that they're trying to get rods down to nothing flat. The time will come when you're not a sportsman unless you use a six-inch tenth-of-an ounce stick. And after that, it'll be merely a long arm. And then trout fishing at the *highest* levels will be restricted to midgets with especially stubby arms—or infants. You'll want to found national associations of 'small fly-fishermen' and 'micro-rodders,' make sassy browns of, say, five inches seem like Atlantic salmon. You're the kind," I told him sternly, "who is ruining the classic art of Skues and Gordon and LaBranche. It's immoral."

He could see that I'd come unhinged and put his arm around my shoulder. "Nicholas, my classic friend," he said, "nothing of the sort is in the offing. Classic I'll never be. I'll still fish for whiting in the dead of winter, at night, on Sheepshead Bay piers; I'll still bounce lead for porgies and flounders in March; I'll still fish for *any* fish anywhere at any time. But I agree in principle with absolutely everything you say about mini-equipment—for regular stream fishing."

"Then why this hang-up?"

"At this very moment, Mr. G. W. Woodville, that master rodmaker, is making me a mini-rod of exactly one foot two and three-tenths inches. Exactly. I *must* have it."

"Clyde, I'm all ears. I've known you for twenty years and not one of your schemes has worked. I remember your plan to stock the East Branch with bluefish. I remember when you showed me that fancy booklet about Mohangolookus Pool on the Rykol River, where 'on a night in June of 1937, the King of Laconia and his two companions killed seventy-three salmon, averaging over twenty pounds.' It was *only* eight thousand dollars per week per beat, including guide, and you didn't make that a year after taxes—and had three children. I remember how you went berserk, sold every last bit of equipment you owned, raised *worms* for sale, conned an agent into a special interim deal, flew to Norway fourth class, hitched to the Rykol River, walked four miles over a small mountain, and finally got to the pool—of which you'd purchased seventy-three minutes' worth for two ninety-eight seventy-five. Clyde, you didn't even have a rod left to fish with!''

"But I saw it,'' he said quietly, flexing the Orvis with obvious affection. "I actually saw Mohangolookus Pool.''

"And now mini-rods?''

"Can't keep it from you, can I?'' he said. "Well, you see this perfectly splendid and logical idea came to me last spring when my wife and three kids and I were ruining a perfectly splendid June afternoon drinking coffee and Cokes in the new vest-pocket Paley Park on Fifty-third Street. The one with the pool and the magnificent falls.

" 'Isn't it lovely?' my wife asked.

" 'Tremendous,' I said. 'Ideal for dries.'

"Well, she shuddered and frowned and insisted that I'd promised the family could have this one day, this one day all that spring together, without me traipsing off with my fishing nuts—no offense—without me even thinking fishing. So I apologized. But then it came to me that perhaps right there in the park wasting such a splendid fly-fishing afternoon other good men like myself were suffering—trapped by insensitive wives and indifferent children who could serenely enjoy themselves in stony Fun City while, two hours away, trout were rising steadily on the Willowemoc. I can feel them, you know. Up to one hundred miles away. Why not stock''—he glanced around and lowered his voice —"why not stock trout in the innumerable little fountains and ponds scattered throughout this asphalt jungle? The aerated water would be cool enough, the water in many of them had sufficient depth . . .''

"*You didn't!*" I said loudly.

He put his finger to his lips. "I envisioned," he went on, serenely, "dapper businessmen stopping by during lunch hours, blithely opening trim little Abercrombie & Fitch traveling cases fitted with trim traveling rods, rigging up, and deftly catching several lunch-hour trout. After an hour of fly-fishing, think of how much more responsible they'd be at their desks!"

"That's true," I had to admit.

"Think of how the millions of trout fishermen who are moving out of this city would return . . ."

"There aren't millions of trout fishermen, thank God."

". . . how the economy of the city would improve and . . ."

"New York has survived, after its fashion, since the Indians without trout," I advised him calmly.

"I'd be the Madison Avenue Walton, the Great Emancipator, beloved by generations of stone-bound anglers the world over, immortalized in song and over Martinis. Never again need there ever be a frustrated angler in New York—nor in any city! A trout in every fountain. Two trout in every fountain. A dozen!" He was beginning to lose control. I thought I saw his eyes roll. "There was the Revlon Fountain at Lincoln Center, the Grand Army Plaza fountains, a perfectly exquisite pond with bubbling waters at the Steuben Glass Building on Fifth Avenue and Fifty-sixth Street, and . . ."

"You're mad, Clyde," I said sadly. "This time you've absolutely lost your marbles. All of them." I took the Orvis from his hands gently. He had begun to shake uncontrollably. Then I gave him a half wave and a shake of my head and started to leave. It might be contagious.

But he grabbed my wrist.

"I decided," he said rapidly, "to start with Paley Park—for sentimental reasons. First I checked with the architect on the size of the falls and the depth of the water. Then I tested the water with my stream thermometer: 58°—perfect. I even got the parks commissioner and the mayor to approve, telling them about the important trout lobby.''

"You actually did it?'' I asked, incredulous. "They're there now? While we're talking?''

"Nope. No, actually they're not there now. Went too far. 'Why not salmon?' I asked myself. And then I had these four perfectly lovely little Atlantic salmon—grilse, actually—flown down from Nova Scotia and stocked them gingerly. Bad mistake. A lapse.''

"I'm all ears.''

"On the third day the salmon suddenly began leaping the falls to Doubleday's; Ed Zern, passing, saw them, went into shock, and nearly caused a nine-car accident. The traffic commissioner came down on me hard.''

"A tragedy, Clyde.''

"They hushed it up, of course. Fearing the trout lobby, no doubt. But I was not to be squelched. Two weeks later, without the approval of the mayor or the parks commissioner or the traffic commissioner, I stocked eleven fat brown trout in the Steuben Glass pool on Fifth Avenue. They took to it beautifully and before work that Tuesday I tried them with my eight-foot Granger.''

"But you couldn't match the city life that was hatching?''

"Nope. Took three on Lady Beaverkills. Dry. But then . . .''

"Don't tell me!''

"Then I caught the Fifth Avenue bus on a back cast.''

I breathed deeply. "They can be damned sporty on light tackle.''

"Nearly got the city struck by the union, that's what! Not one of the 'assumed hazards,' they said. Needed an increase to cover it. But that's why I'm having this one-foot two-and-three-tenths-inch rod made.''

"So you can fish the Steuben Glass fountain again?''

"Nope.''

"All right, I'll bite. The Revlon Fountain? The fountains at the Metropolitan Museum? Downtown or uptown?''

"I see you've been looking, too.''

I frowned.

"Couple of weeks ago," he said confidentially, "I poached a box of good stream life out of the Beaverkill and dropped it into the Seal Pool in Central Park along with a half-dozen mixed browns and brookies."

"*Nooooo*, Clyde. You didn't!"

"I've been watching it, Nick," he said. "There are ab-so-lute-ly superb hatches in the evening and I plan to sneak in a dozen or so casts tomorrow at lunch hour. I'm getting the mini-rod so I won't catch any stray kiddies. Hooking one of those would be worse than catching a union bus."

I'd had enough. "Good luck," I muttered. And under my breath: "May your leaders rot and save you imprisonment, old Clyde."

And then I left rapidly. It was catching.

I met him several weeks later on Madison Avenue. He had a large bag under his arm and was headed for Abercrombie's. He was ecstatic. "What're they taking, Clyde?" I asked, taking his shoulder affectionately.

"Cow Dung," he whispered. "Twelves and fourteens—barbless."

"Where?" I whispered back.

"Won't tell anyone?" He paused. "Seal Pool."

"You're kidding!"

"Took two last night," he said matter-of-factly.

"*Trout?* In Central Park? You *really* took two?" I was suffering from a bit of trout deprivation myself, and the thought unhinged me.

"No, the seals got the trout before I could, of course—should have figured. But I took two small seals on a number fourteen Cow Dung right at dusk. God, what a fight they give on a mini-rod! My only worry was that truck that came around just as I released the second. Had on it, ASPCA. Are seals fish?"

"Mammals, Clyde," I said, recovering quickly. "And they're out of season. You're lucky the truck didn't say Bellevue. Perhaps we could just sit down, Clyde, old man, and talk this out. I'm starting a local chapter of Anglers Anonymous—when you feel this coming on again, just phone me, any time of the day or night, Clyde, and . . ."

"Oh, come on, friend," he snapped nervously. "If I don't get over to Abercrombie's, this bag of ice cubes is going to melt all over Madison Avenue. I don't much appreciate being humored. Certainly not by *you*."

Somewhere in his last words was a straight line, but I couldn't grasp it.

"Look," he said hoarsely, "we just have time to get this ice up to the A & F roof and get down to the ninth floor. We'll hide in the sail loft until they close. Then . . ."

Even when seized by the vapors, anglers seem to have a subliminal sense of communication—or, as they say, it takes one to know one. "Clyde, you don't mean . . ."

"Exactly!" he shouted, grasping my arm. "The casting pool on the roof."

He reached in his pocket and shakily withdrew a bill of lading marked Alaska Airways. He held it close to my face.

"Since lunchtime today, pal," he announced triumphantly. "Stocked with Arctic grayling."

7

The Fine Art of Hudson River Fence Fishing

 FLY CASTING ON THE NEW-MOWN GRASS in Riverside Park, I was pleased to see a fellow brother of the angle walk briskly through the crowd of skeptical onlookers. He had an army carryall slung on his shoulder and a long and heavy saltwater rod in his hand; his nose was bright red and there was a pint bottle stashed neatly in the back pocket of his baggy gabardines. *Stenonema fuscum* had appeared on the Schoharie, my scouts had reported, but I had only caught a half-dozen good clumps of fresh-cut grass in an hour of serious casting. They were about five or six inches apiece, I suppose, and I had slipped them off the unbarbed and, in fact, untipped yellow fly easily. They gave no appreciable fight.

"You never ketch 'em here," the angler advised, with a loud laugh.

"Where're *you* going?"

"The river." He came over and shook his head at my bamboo fly rod.

"What do you get?" I asked.

"Fish," he said. "What you get with toot-pick?"

"Grass," I replied.

He waved his hand down, laughed loudly again, and then, somewhat surreptitiously I thought, marched quickly off. I had seen that particular step before. It was somewhat too determined and hurried. A telltale phenomenon. The man had information that he was keeping from his brothers. Was there a striper run on? Could shad be in the river and available to the initiate? Herring?

My four children were with me and we had an intolerably long June afternoon, hot and landlocked in the city, stretched in front of us. Even Clyde was in the Catskills.

Why not, I thought: I'll try the river.

I sent Paul back for his spinning rod and Charles to the fish market on Broadway for twenty-five cents' worth of squid. Pier fishing, if that's what it was to be, was not new to me. When I was a kid I'd bike down to Sheepshead or Steeplechase piers and fish for porgies, ling, whiting, blowfish, hackleheads, and whatever else could be scared up from the bottom. Most of them had scared me—with their horns and prickles, their ignoble inflating and deflating. It was a weird business, practiced in snow and boiling sun, and I had not regretted relinquishing it when I fell in love with trout—which at least had no horns and only grew fat in one's imagination. I had never tried the Hudson, though we lived only a block away, in the center of Manhattan. A slide presentation by Bob Boyle at the Theodore Gordon Flyfishers' dinner in March had intrigued me with the fecundity of the river, and I had, years before, caught stripers and even herring on flies as far north as Barrytown.

Without disjointing my fly rod, I took my two young ones by the hands and headed for the river. Twenty minutes later the spinning rod and squid arrived, and I was ready for action.

It was an exquisite day.

The sun was bright, the sky was pleasantly flecked with soft white-grey clumps of clouds. The New Jersey palisades were firm, angular, and green. A couple of posh cabin cruisers headed upriver; a long brown barge headed down. Several women were sunbathing against the slope of the hill; they had hardly any clothes on; one of them was more angular and firm than the palisades. A helicopter fluttered up the mighty Hudson like a bloated swallow—but found no mayflies rising.

I saw at once that this was not pier but *fence* fishing. There were some eighteen or twenty anglers spread along a hundred yards of fence. Their heavy saltwater rods were leaned at precisely the same angle against the railing, and all of them were standing back ten to twenty feet, alone or in little groups. There was one spirited group of eight to ten Puerto Ricans whose lively chatter rose above their loud radio music.

I found an unoccupied few yards, laid my fly rod carefully against the fence, set up the spinning rod, cut and threaded on a slab of squid, and cast out. I have never been the sort to leave a rod unattended—neither on the forked sticks common to reservoir fishing nor on piers—so I held it lightly couched in my arm, with my right index finger pressing against the monofilament. I even gave the line a few sporadic tugs, to impart some action.

After an hour, my older boys grew bored and went off to play baseball; Jennifer and Anthony ran to investigate the boat basin a couple of hundred yards downriver. I had experienced my share of family disasters while trying to fish for trout, and was enormously grateful that they could thus occupy themselves. I had perhaps discovered an anglers' paradise in the midst of grey New York. There were escape facilities for the children, music (if that's what you wanted), company, a beautiful landscape across the river, shapely sunbathers; there was no wasted time getting to the fishing grounds; there would be no anxiety lest the day's hatch be missed, or go unmatched. If it wasn't the Schoharie when the Hendricksons were on, and you were alone with fish feeding in every run and pocket, it was still—I rationalized—a line in the water.

But I soon discovered that Hudson River fence fishing is an art not to be taken lightly—an art with its own traditions and lore, its own ethics and mores; it is also essentially a traditionalist's art, for I'll wager there have been few changes over the past seventy years—nor any tolerance or encouragement paid the rebel. Innovation, as for the fabled lotus-eaters on the Beaverkill, is met with distrust bordering on disgust.

At precisely 3:27, one of the Puerto Rican anglers let out a momentous howl, not unlike that of the hound of the Baskervilles. He raced down the slope, grasped his rod, and struck it back five feet. *"Grande, grande!"* he shouted, and was soon surrounded by seven or eight onlookers. He reeled his line in without hesitation, with a sweep of his arm heaved his fish directly out, and a moment later there was a long green eel flapping and squiggling on the grass.

An interesting tool was then produced, which I had never seen used before. It looked to me like a piece of twisted wire hanger. It was carefully placed just ahead of the hook, with eel hanging down. Then, with an abrupt movement, the eel was flipped in a circle around the tool. Whatever was supposed to happen did not. The maneuver was nevertheless tried again and this time the eel came quickly and miraculously off the hook and flopped to the ground. There it was ceremoniously kicked at and stabbed with a long knife until it lay motionless. A mutt was brought near, but it showed singular disinterest in the long corpse.

Then a general query was raised whether anyone wanted the remains. There was no response and the eel was thereafter handled meanly by several children—until it disappeared.

I asked one of the men the name of the instrument used to disgorge the hook so handily. "Wire," he replied.

Soon another cry went up and another young man raced to his rod. Within the next twenty minutes another and then another rod were struck back fiercely, and four more eels were swiftly brought to fence. The rise was going full blast and, frankly, I felt somewhat left out. I reeled in my strip of squid and discovered it to be singularly unmolested. Anthony had returned and I asked him to seek out a good angler willing to part with a few worms—for that, I had now substantiated, was what they were rising (or sinking) to; I gave him a quarter and made him swear not to spend it for ice cream. He acquired four night crawlers (though bloodworms are considered slightly superior), and I promptly threaded a whole one onto my #10 Eagle Claw hook.

I continued to hold my rod and in a few minutes was rewarded with a few faint but telltale taps.

I must have been overanxious, this being my first eel, for I struck quickly and came up with a shredded worm.

My second strike came at 4:27. I gave this one more time, but again came up with only a mutilated worm and a long strip of tissue paper.

Several other eels had meanwhile been caught, and also one striped bass. My field notes concerning the striper read as follows:

Striper caught at 4:20. Bait: worm. Size: about seven inches. Fight: negligible. Miscellaneous comments: Angler claimed: "Got one about the same size, same time, day before yesterday." May be significant. Fish stashed quickly in bottom of metal box.

Soon after I missed my second strike, I realized that much more careful thought was necessary if I were to master this art. Careful observation is indispensable to the serious angler, and I soon noted the following: no other angler was holding his rod. In fact, there seemed a deliberate attempt not even to notice it. The fishermen would stand in a crowd, and then, either by instinct born of long experience, by sight, or from the tinkling sound of one of the small bells attached to the tip of many a rod, they would leap to the fence for action. The Hudson River fence strike is sudden and abrupt, delivered with killing force; I presume this is to compensate for the bend the river must put in the line, though it may simply be the natural hostility of urbanites.

There seems to be the widest latitude concerning the proper clothing for this kind of fishing. Short pants, Havana shirts (not tucked in), or no shirts, and leather moccasins appeared to prevail; though I observed four or five anglers in traditional street clothes. I could come to no conclusion concerning the logic for dress, and must assume my subsequent failures were in no way related to what I wore—khaki trousers, an Orvis vest, and my slouch stream hat.

I queried several fishermen who had displayed conspicuous success. Their characteristic mode of expression was laconic, authoritative, unequivocal. The following conversation transpired:

"Ever use plugs?" I asked.

"Nope."

"Spoons?"

"Nope."

"Any kind of artificial lure?"

"Nope."

"Why not?"

"No good."

"Have you tried them?"

"Waste of time."

I had noticed that one fisherman spit on the bit of worm he affixed to his hook, and asked him: "Why do you do that?"

"It helps."

"Ever catch anything on top?"

"Nope."

The angler I'd met in the park made me his confidant. He was extremely knowledgeable and perhaps felt some sympathy for me because I seemed to try so hard, I had two small children who were by now embarrassed at my ineptness, because anyone who used toot-picks was in need of counsel, and perhaps because he had been the instrument of my conversion. Taking me under his wing, he promptly advised that I would never catch a thing if I persisted in holding the rod.

"You ketch 'em in the country like that, maybe; not here. See these places?" He pointed to some old notches in the railing; I had not seen them before. "You put rod there."

I was tempted to ask him precisely why, in order to learn whether these long green ropes were so tender-lipped that they could sense the presence of a fisherman, but he was intent upon imparting a great deal of information to me quickly, in order to get back to his bottle of Old Grand-dad, so I let him go on. I was not at all sure such an opportunity would present itself again. If he were indeed a deputy of the Castle, a secretary of the curia, I would not be caught napping.

"Your weight no good; you need three, maybe four ounces." I was using about a half ounce of split shot, pinched on and strung along a foot of line. It seemed to hold the bottom, and the spinning rod could not manage anything heavier. I told him so.

"You never ketch 'em," he told me flatly.

Spiritually, I could not quite work my way around to the four ounces.

"Your bait wrong," he said. "You need him little piece of worm, like this." He squashed off about a half inch of worm and was about to put it on my hook. Before I could tell him that I had always, in my salad days when I fished worms, done better with a whole bait, he added: "No. No. Hook wrong, too. You need long hook. I get you one."

This was downright decent of him, but I thought I could get them just as well on a short-shank hook and told him so. He shook his head and was about to give me up when I asked him: "Tell me the truth. Why don't any of you guys hold the rod?"

"No good."

"Don't you *like* to feel the fish biting?"

He roared with laughter and took my rod. "You hold this," he said, giving it to me.

I took the rod back.

"Now put finger on line." He gave the line at the end a few small twitches and then broke up laughing. I had to agree that this element of the sport had little enough to recommend it.

Since I had seen my friend keep several eels, I asked him if he ate them.

"Sure," he said.

"Even from the Hudson?"

I might as well have cursed his mother. He said nothing.

"Well, how do you cook them?"

He came over close to me and whispered: "You put nail in his head, then strip skin off, cut him in chunks and fry or stew him."

"Easy as that?"

"You stew him like beef stew." He made several facial expressions indicating gastronomical happiness.

When he left me, I condescended to put a bit of worm on my wrong hook and cast it out. Then I went back to the grass and lay down on the slope, closing my eyes against the warm redness of the sun, listening to the pleasantly rhythmic chatter, and thinking back a month to a May afternoon when the Hendricksons were popping up out of a still pool in the Catskills and riding slowly downriver like little sailboats until they were sucked under, dramatically, by the trout. A sparsely tied Red Quill, with genuine blue dun hackle, had done some happy business for me.

I was on my third trout when I heard Jennifer shout: "Our ball's in the water, Dad." They had been playing nearby. I got up slowly and went over to the fence. A tennis ball was bobbing slowly along the rim of the rocks. It belonged to the son of one of the regulars.

There was some immediate interest in this, and four or five of the more agile anglers hopped the fence and vied for the honor of fishing the ball out. One of them got way out on a rock and with a long stick proceeded to prod at the ball. It only bobbed under and farther out.

"What are those?" Jennifer asked, leaning far over the railing and pointing.

I looked. "Balloons."

"Oh."

The young man with the stick was now holding onto his companion's arm with one hand and leaning still farther out.

"Look," said Jennifer. "More balloons."

There were two more. "There must be a party upriver," I told her.

"Can we go?" asked Anthony.

"Look, he's got the ball," I said.

The young man had indeed dropped his stick and grasped the ball, but as he did so his foot slipped against the slippery rocks and he careened over into the river. Rather than alarm, this caused numerous shouts and cheers and considerable excitement. The man went under once, losing his baseball cap, splashed and shouted with animation—as one might, say, if he had fallen into a sewer—and then got a hand on the rocks, forced himself up by sheer will, and was finally lifted out.

There was mucho celebration.

But then it was noticed that his hat was gone.

Several men reeled in their lines and tried to probe for it with the rods, but only managed to push it farther out. Finally it got some twenty feet out into the river, with only a bit of the peak showing.

One good turn deserved another, so I reeled in my line, took off the half inch of worm, pushed the split shot down flush with the hook, and made several short underhand casts. I could not hook the cap.

Then I saw the fly rod.

While the hat was ever so slowly moving farther away, I clipped off my yellow practice fly and tied on a #8 Eagle Claw hook. Then, stripping line off my reel, and to the utter amazement of all the onlookers, I began to false cast. They watched in silence as the white line sailed back and then forward.

On the third cast, I was able to lay my line over the hat, and then, drawing it slowly in by hand was lucky enough to catch the hook onto some part of it. Alternately filling with water and losing water through the air holes in the top, and hooked but lightly, the cap rode in majestically across the majestic waters of the Hudson. It took some care and strategy to bring it to the rocks and then up and over the fence. At its best weight, the cap went a full two pounds, I guess, and gave a good account of itself.

The landing was watched with muted silence, and then, when the hat was safely landed, the event was greeted with what I took to be somewhat extravagant praise. I was toasted, congratulated, invited to share in the community bottle, and offered a long, thin, green rope, which had once been an eel.

It was late now, and I took my toot-pick and headed hand in hand with my young ones up the hill. A cool breeze had come on, and the near-naked ladies had long since left; the globed sun was cherry red and serrated with soft Payne's grey clouds. I could smell the new-mown grass and listened to the sweet methodical hum of cars on the West Side Highway.

At home a patient fishing widow waited, one who, like me, had never reckoned with the special delights of Hudson River fence fishing. Fortunately, I doubt if I can ever master this art. But it is well to remember that there's more than one way to skin a cat—or an eel.

HOW TO GET THERE: All major airlines fly to Kennedy, Newark, and LaGuardia airports. All regular train and bus lines come directly to New York City. The #5 Riverside Drive bus stops on the corner of West Eighty-third Street. Crosstown buses at Eighty-sixth and Seventy-ninth. Seventh Avenue subway. Do not come by car—parking not available.

BEST TIME: Same catches reported all year long. Come when you can.

ACCOMMODATIONS: Great latitude—from Waldorf-Astoria to nearby furnished rooms. Rat traps a necessity if you choose the latter.

COSTS: Will vary greatly; generally astronomical.

CONTACTS: Ask for Joe at the Eighty-fourth Street fence.

WHAT TO TAKE: Bring cheapest and heaviest saltwater tackle; four- and five-ounce sinkers; #8 long-shank hooks; a couple of night crawlers or bloodworms will last a day; all clothing acceptable. Transistor radios useful.

ADDITIONAL INFORMATION: Literature on Hudson River fence fishing is currently unavailable. No books on subject now in print, though it is probable dozens will be written in the coming years.

Part Two

FATHERS AND SONS,
WOMEN AND RIVERS

8

The Nine-Pound Bass

EVERY EVENING THAT SUMMER AFTER I had finished waiting on tables I would grab up my tackle from the green metal locker and head for the lake. The campers, stuffed and content from the mountains of food I had helped serve them for supper, would be back on the hill, leaving the docks and canoes and the lake—so wildly busy all day—to me. The lake would be glass-flat and dark. Alone and often bone tired, I would stand on the docks or sit in the bow of a silently gliding canoe and cast for the fat black bass that were just beginning to take their supper.

Along the brushy shorelines of the lake, schools of small shiners scurried and flipped along the surface, ruffling it like a breeze, a black bass in hungry pursuit. Bugs dropped from the overhanging pine and hemlock and birch branches, and you could see the water open with a momentous and heart-stopping *woompt*.

During the day the campers dominated the four-mile lake—swimming and canoeing, splashing and shouting and thrashing its green waters white. In the evening the lake was still and calm and mine.

I loved to glide slowly past the shoreline, some forty to fifty feet out, and cast my surface plugs and poppers in against the rocks and pads and bring them back with soft ploops and slurps. The stillness was hypnotic and only abetted by the rhythmic motion of my arm, casting and retrieving, casting carefully and bringing the lure in with a calculated sensuality. The bass cracked the stillness with quick explosive charges; they crashed up at the lure, overwhelmed it, leapt far into the air, shaking high and wildly.

My only companions that July were two Chinese, a cook and a baker's helper who often came down an hour after I'd started and sat side by side on the whitewashed docks and fished with handlines for sunfish, perch, and bullheads. They used bread kneaded into small balls and were quiet and skillful at their craft; they often half filled a pail with their mixed catch in a couple of hours of silent work.

They spoke a few words of English, but mostly confined themselves to indefinite shouts of praise when they saw me connect, from the dock or far out on the lake, with a good bass. Then they'd stand and clap and cry: "Beeg fishee, velly beeg fishee." And when I came over to where they were, after a spirited tussle, they'd clap their hands on my back, nod their heads, and handle the fish with admiration. It was not the sort of fish they expected to catch, and they respected my talent with the rod and my success: so much, in fact, that I got exceptionally good care in the kitchen, was saved choice pieces of meat and the best cakes, and gained eight pounds that July.

Those evenings were pure and serene and solitary, filled with a quiet the more valued after a long day of noisy work in the scorching kitchen, plopping salt tablets down my throat a couple an hour, helping to stuff four hundred campers who had paid for the best. The three of us would stand on the dock for hours without a sound—listening to the splash of shiners and bass nearby or far out on the darkening lake, the occasional grunt from my companions when they pulled up a "velly" nice perch or bull-head, the ploop and slurp of a popper working its way across a channel among lily pads, the sweet crashing sound of a good large-mouth erupting out of the still lake. It was worth all the insolence of my offices.

We even had drama—for a huge submarine of a bass would occasionally meander near the dock, and we would all gawp and try for it. It was the largest freshwater fish I'd ever seen, the size of a cod or a striper or a blue, and he roamed contentedly in the area between the lily pads and the dock. We saw him regularly, once or twice a week. I tried for him every day, when I went by canoe or fished from the dock—first and last. He was an unhurried and wise old bastard and never gave me the slightest turn or look. He was our greatest challenge and our private goad, and I longed to feel him on my line, to see the water of our evening idyll erupt massively with his bull force. I tried for him first and last, but never for more than a few moments—for he was so singularly in-accessible. But I would have given anything to take him. Anything.

And then the serpent entered our garden.

It happened one evening in late July. She was about five-four, quite slim and busty, and had extraordinary, soft auburn hair. The assistant girl's swimming instructor had gotten chicken pox and then married, and this creature had taken her place.

I saw her first when I came down in my sneakers, on the run, bait-casting rod and small metal tackle box in either hand, one Monday evening. The weekend had been particularly busy, with guests up who had to be fed until nine o'clock, and I had done no fishing whatsoever for two whole days.

I came racehorsing down the hill, hoping the monster would be there at the end of the dock, moving in his unhurried course toward or away from the lily pads, when I saw her lying on her back, in her bathing suit, breathing heavily in and out. Dumb-founded, I dropped my metal box. It clattered on the boards and she turned quickly toward me, frightened. I was not less so.

She had only been doing breathing exercises, and we were

soon good friends. Quite good. The next evening I did not hesitate to put aside my rod and take her to a local square dance. I generally hated barn dances but my feet touched no straw that night: she had knocked them from under me. Her name was Valerie.

We saw each other regularly for two weeks and naturally I did no bass fishing whatsoever. By the time I had gotten to know her well enough to disclose my deepest sins and passions, my love for angling, the Chinese were scarcely speaking to me anymore. They thought I was lost. They gave me little more than deferential nods; they shook their heads; they whispered in Chinese behind my back. "No likee chickee," the baker's assistant told me bluntly.

Nevertheless, the cook was good enough to inform me one evening, after I'd come back for a third order of potatoes for one of my tables, that the "velly beeg bas'erd" had been seen the previous night. "Velly beeg," he assured me. "Velly *velly* beeg fishee."

There were no dances that night and I thought Valerie might be amused by an evening on the docks, so, rather sheepishly, I decided to show her that final recess of my heart: the angler. She was an adventuresome girl in many pleasant ways and always anxious to learn something new. When I proposed it to her, she said: "Show me, Nicky."

I promised to bring down a spare rod and did so. We were to meet on the dock. I arrived first and the Chinese were delighted to see me: they clapped me on the back like a friend arrived from the dead and chattered excitedly. But when Valerie appeared, they mumbled something in Chinese that sounded like a curse or a threat and hunched glumly over their handlines.

For myself, in retrospect, I had a bittersweet evening that makes me blush to recall it. There I stand, arm pleasantly around her shoulder, moving her wrist back and forth rhythmically.

"What happens next?" she asks.

I move her wrist a dozen times without explanation. "You let go," I say.

"Of the rod?"

"Your thumb. When the rod gets to this position—three o'clock—release the line."

She does so, but too late, and the plug crashes into the water five yards from the boat.

"Not bad," I mumble, looking at the bird's nest in the reel.

"What's this?" she asks.

"Bird's nest," I say.

"Is that bad?"

"It's terrible."

She roars and hugs me. I hug her back. She is warm and compelling and much more interesting than a bird's nest. The Chinese shout Chinese epithets at us and point. We nearly fall off the dock together.

"Why don't I just undo this now?" I say, undoing myself and sitting down. My knees are weak.

"Do you *have* to?"

"We came to fish."

"Yes," she says, at once serious, "and I'd really like to learn, Nicky."

It takes a half hour to undo the knots. She giggles and kisses my neck. I show her how to cast and on my first cast get my first bird's nest in five years. It takes me another half hour to undo the second bird's nest. She troubles me the whole time. I am about to cast again but she stops me. She gently puts the rod down, kisses me, and sends us both off the dock and—with a momentous *whoompt*—into the water. The Chinese are delirious with venom and leave, cursing.

But Valerie soon proved a compulsive learner. She could not have cared less about fishing, about the *heart* of fishing, I'm sure, but she was a better swimmer than I and most young men my age, she was a better tennis player I'd learned one miserable afternoon, and now she wanted to be a better fisherman. That, of course, was ridiculous, and I told her so.

"I was born fishing," I told her. "I've been fishing since I was an infant. I dream about rivers and lakes. I move my casting arm in my sleep. Anyway, you're too pretty to be a good fisherman. It takes natural recluses and outcasts like the Chinese and me.

"What's so hard?" she asked. And she began to practice like a demon. I even loaned her one of my rods so she could practice from the dock between swimming classes. With her long fingers she soon became expert at picking apart bird's nests. In another week the skill was obsolete: she didn't get bird's nests anymore and was beginning to drop the popper off the tips of the lily pads at sixty-five feet. I must have seen the handwriting: I asked for my rod back.

It was by now late August. Every evening we would meet at the dock and automatically head out in one of the canoes, I paddling from the bow, she fishing from the comfortable middle seat. It was a compulsive, intense ritual. I was fascinated by her. My lures would hang up in the lily pads; I'd get bird's nests with alarming regularity and she wouldn't even stop to help me undo them; I couldn't keep my eyes off her; she caught bass after bass, though—as I pointed out—mostly small ones, smaller than my few horses.

She was a natural. She was all I had dreamed of throughout my teens: beautiful, sensuous, and a deft bait caster. She even treated it like the art it was—though I always suspected hers was a mechanistic art, devoid of the true feeling of the initiate. Like all arts, it took its toll: exhausted after long hours on the dock teaching swimming and long evening hours intently casting her poppers, when we came off the lake she would go directly to her cabin. Alone. You can't have your cake and eat it. I didn't know whether to cheer or cry. Had the summer lasted much longer I would merely have collapsed.

It did not. The night of the final banquet I had arranged to meet her at the dock as soon as I finished serving. I knew she would be there early since she did not have a group of children to care for and I would be tied up until nearly dusk. We intended to fish late, until ten or eleven.

The dinner was a sweat-trap and I emerged a limp rag. I showered quickly, changed into fresh clothes, and got to the dock about eight forty-five. There I saw an incredible sight: Valerie and the Chinese were doing a wild jig, their hands on each others' shoulders, on the corner of the dock. They were ecstatic. They were jubilant. They were triumphant. When I came closer I saw over what. It was the bass—huge and bronze, barnacled and antique—flopping listlessly on the white boards in the cool grey dusk. She had taken it on a live sunfish, hooked through the dorsal. On a handline!

The Chinese wanted me to marry this "velly nice chickee" on the spot. They implored me to do so.

I took back my rod and never spoke to her again.

The fish weighed exactly nine pounds four ounces; I've never taken one larger.

9

In a Barrel

IT HAD BEEN A SIZABLE TROUT, OVER fourteen inches, and he had taken it by himself on a spinning rod and a lure from a small clear Catskill creek. Its silhouette, carefully marked out on brown butcher paper, took its place beside basketball heroes, favorite poems, maps, and the Karsh photo of Hemingway on his wall. It is no small matter to take a first trout.

The second was more reluctant.

The boy did not take a fish on our next five outings. There were endless hang-ups, snarls, quick strikes and late strikes, lost hooks, lost bait, cold feet, hot head—everything I had gone through, alone, while I was learning. Everything every fisherman has gone through—for is it not one of the most persnickety arts to learn well? I knew that he had to go through it, yet I was afraid he would lose his feeling, his heart for the game—and that I would lose a deeply valued streamside companion whom I had waited nine long years to fish with.

It was a serious matter and I was giving it all a good worry when he announced one day that he wanted me to take him and two of his friends trout fishing for his birthday. No circus, no movie, no party: trout fishing.

The spark was too good to lose.

And yet my knowledge of his two young friends assured me that they had no experience and little interest, and that I would spend a long afternoon in birds' nests, climbing trees and fearing for wildly thrown lures, changing spools and hooks and bait endlessly—and we wouldn't get a thing. That was the worst of it: an afternoon in June with spinning lures and worms and three nine-year-olds augured no good. It would be frustrating and fruitless.

But since he would take no substitutes and had already announced the day to his friends, I finally agreed. Should I take them to the Beaverkill or the Esopus? The Ten Mile or the East Branch? Or perhaps some safe reservoir bank—for white perch, crappies, and pumpkinseeds? Perhaps that would be best. At least there would be some action. Paul insisted it had to be trout and I resigned myself to the worst of it.

Then, several days before we were to leave, I learned of a trout farm about two hours upstate. A neighbor told me cheerfully, in passing, that you could not help but catch 'em there. That had to be the answer. It was guaranteed.

We stowed our gear like good sportsmen and headed up at a leisurely hour. The kids were all questions for the first ten minutes: no more. Then they were all over each other like restless puppies. I kept remarking on how lovely a day it was, but they could see outside only when they came loose from their wrestling in the back of the car.

I came off the Quickway two stops too late, but didn't lose more than fifteen minutes. What was the hurry? Perhaps I'd simply let them fight out the birthday! They seemed to enjoy that well enough. But they came out of the backseat arena in time to point out a WORMS sign and I promptly stopped there and bought sixty cents' worth of insurance: it was the bargain of the day.

We got to the farm about 2:00, I paid the fifty cents admission per person—which seemed cheap enough: this might even prove to be one of the cheaper birthdays—and we scurried in with our armfuls of gear.

Several conspicuous signs caught my attention immediately. They are, I believe, self-explanatory.

ALL FISH CAUGHT *MUST* BE KEPT!
CUTTING LINES *NOT* PERMITTED!
YOU *MUST* USE A NET!

I was impressed with the forcefulness of these instructions: they were singularly without equivocation. But I did think they stressed certain unsportsmanlike qualities.

There was also a typewritten sheet, quite a bit smaller, on which all of the above instructions were reiterated and on which, if one looked quite closely, could be found the phrase *"Two dollars per pound."*

Two dollars a pound! There were four of us. What if we caught ten trout apiece. I could buy an Orvis for that. An Orvis! The lovely eight-foot Battenkill I'd been brooding on all year long.

The water was merely a bull-dozed pond a couple of acres around. It was fed by a tiny creek, but the current disappeared almost immediately. Not a fish showed on the surface. I was elated. Perhaps if there were a few trout in this sump they were small.

"Is *this* it?" asked Paul.

"There aren't any fish in there at all," said John.

"Looks terrific," I said. "Let's get rigged."

I had no sooner finished setting up Bill and thrown his line in than the rod arched over sharply. He was into a darn good fish.

"Hold him, Bill. Don't reel too quickly. Don't force him. He's a good one."

Bill was shouting and jumping up and down. I thought he'd break that glass spinning rod, the arc was so great. Paul and John were excited, too, and tugged at me to get their lines in also. I rigged them, as simultaneously as possible, and they both cast out quickly.

In a moment, they too had fish on their lines.

I was impressed by the obvious size of the fish. Not one had showed yet, but they were obviously three- or four-dollar trout. At a minimum. In a few moments, I noticed that Bill's fish was tiring and I picked up a nearby net to help him. The size of the fish as I lifted it stunned me: it was a fine fat rainbow, fully more than two pounds, possibly close to three. The others soon got theirs on high ground also. We had about seven, eight pounds of fish in the first five minutes: it was an awesome business.

I baited them all up quickly and this time they had to wait for a full and tiring three or four minutes before they got strikes. Fortunately, Paul and Bill struck late and wasted two worms. I helped the situation by tossing in four or five juicy crawlers, side-arm.

"What're you doing that for?" asked John.

"To chum 'em up," I said. "Action seems to have slowed down."

Where the worms dropped the water boiled as if piranhas were in the pond.

Then a young chap came around to see that we weren't cutting any lines or throwing back any fish or fishing with any barbless hooks, and I took the opportunity to ask him if there was any bug life in the pond and whether or not these trout ever took flies. When I saw the size of those fish I had unhoused my old Granger and was hoping to get one of them on: they were huge fish, gave a good account of themselves despite the sluggish water, and if I was going to go broke that afternoon I should be able to treat myself to one of them on the long rod. It's a jaded angler indeed who can pass up trout that size, even if they are in a barrel.

"No hatches, if that's what you mean," the young native told me. "But some guys do pretty well on a greenish fly just below the surface."

"Greenish? You mean a nymph?"

"Not exactly. Doesn't really make much difference what it

represents, so long as it's fairly small—like so—and green.''

"Well, what kind of creature is it supposed to represent?''

"No creature. We feed these fish green pellets.''

"*Green* pellets?''

"Yup. Green as grass, and about so big.'' He held up two fingers again, so that if I was up to it I could match the hatch properly.

"Guess I'll sit this one out,'' I said, disjointing my rod. "I've never been able to tie a satisfactory Pellet Fly.''

"Suit yourself, if you wanna let the kids have all the fun.''

The boys had taken three trout among them by now, and I noted with satisfaction that there were only four worms left. One of these was lengthening himself out of the can, and I let him, always an encourager of independence and exploration, marveling at his ingenuity and praising him silently for his thoughtfulness.

When the boys saw that there were only three worms left, they decided to use halfies—but I told them emphatically that these would never catch any self-respecting trout, not even these rabid pellet gobblers.

Finally there was only one live worm left. Bill and John had taken another horse each, making eight trout between them; Paul had three. Eleven whales. The good young man was standing by, if not to advise me further, then certainly to see that we didn't smuggle out any three-dollar trout in our pants' legs. I'm sure he heard my mind calculating wildly. I told Bill and John that four was the limit.

Paul had the last worm and soon got a solid strike. But he was overanxious and hauled away too quickly. The worm came up shredded but was good enough, I thought, to catch one of these wise old starving bows.

Apparently it wasn't.

Or else the school, yea the university, had moved away from the devastating harvesters. For in six casts he didn't even get a touch. This at first pleased me. But then I saw that he was anxious to get four fish like his friends. They had grown bored by inaction —we'd been there all of a half hour and they'd only caught four fish larger than I'd take in five full seasons of fly-fishing.

"Hurry up, Paul," said John.

"I'm bored, Paul. Can't you catch one?"

Paul cast hard, flinging the shredded worm off.

"Well, I guess that does it, kids," I said. "But we've got quite a load of fish here. I'll bet there are over twenty-five pounds of trout in that basket."

"*Please* let me catch another, Dad," said Paul.

I asked the young man if they sold worms and he said that they were out. So I told Paul to try a little silver lure, and let him tie it on himself. He did so carefully and looked up to me for approval. But he was still casting too hard and long and retrieving with too much impatience and speed.

"Aw, come on, Paul. You can't catch one. We're better fishermen than you any day."

"You'll never get one on that piece of metal, Paul. That's not good for catching trout. Anyone can see that."

I said that it was—that it was too deadly and ought to be outlawed. But Paul could get nothing on it, and I could see that he was growing even more upset so I went over to a little grassy plot and dug around with a stick trying to find a few little worms. There were none, and when I came back a few minutes later I could see that the boys were really razzing him now.

"Boys, boys," I said. "There's no need to do that. Maybe the fish have just stopped biting. Why don't we leave now? We have more than enough fish."

"Please," said Paul. "One more. I'll get one. I know I will, Dad. I know I will."

But try as he might, he could not.

He was fishing intently now, eyeing the water with real concentration; he even let his lure go very low and retrieved it with slower, sharp jerks—a deadly method in lakes. I took the opportunity to send the other two over to get Cokes. They were delighted with the idea.

"I've got to get one, Dad. I've just *got* to."

"My son, my son. There's no competition involved in fishing. There shouldn't be. It has nothing to do with what anyone else has caught. You've got three good ones. I didn't get any. I didn't even get to fish."

Paul tried two more casts and then, with a bit of a sad sigh and a holding up of his chest, said: "OK, Dad. I'm ready. We can go now."

Late that night, after I had dropped the other children home with their mammoth trout, I went up to Paul's room to say goodnight.

"You know, Dad," he said, "I like to catch really big fish like that, and these were the biggest I've ever caught, bigger than my first one there on the wall, but you don't like that kind of fishing, do you?"

"No, son. I like to catch native trout, when they're hard to take, when you can take them on flies—and I don't have to pay for them."

"These got pretty hard to take," he said, smiling.

"They certainly did. Gosh, that was some situation there. All the kids heckling you and you not catching a thing. I'll bet I couldn't have caught a fish then either."

"That's all right, Dad. I got three very big trout and that's more than you ever come home with."

I laughed. "You're absolutely right. Well, I like to get out on the stream by myself, or with one good friend, or with my son Aloysius P. T. McPaul, look at the water a little, watch the flies that are coming off, tell a few big fish tales, fish a little, and maybe catch a few and maybe throw back a few."

"I like to catch a lot of fish."

"And you will. You handle that rod very well, and you'll handle a fly rod well, too."

And then I turned off the light and patted his back for a few moments and talked about hatches and flies and big fish I'd seen, and big ones I'd missed, and he said, "You know, Dad, I'm glad we went and all that, and I'm glad you took me there for my birthday like I asked, but a birthday is really a different kind of day, isn't it, like the Fourth of July or a circus? And what I'd really like is to go up to the Beaverkill or someplace like that, like you're always bothering Mom about, and do some *real* trout fishing"

"We will, we will, my son."

"Next weekend?"

"Perhaps not so soon. But before long. I'd like to do that very very much."

"So would I, Dad. Just the two of us. So there's no competition or anything like that."

"I wouldn't be the slightest bit of competition for you," I said. And then I patted his back some more and tucked the little feller in, and just before he closed his eyes he turned to me and said: "Dad, that was no better than catching them in a barrel, was it?"

10

On the Divide

FOR THREE DAYS WE FISHED THE LAKE without a strike. We rose each morning at four, dressed quickly by the bald light of the bulb in the kitchen of the cabin, and then carried our rods and tackle bags silently through the darkness, down the hill, and to the aluminum boat.

The motor started only once on the first pull of the cord. Neither of us was adept at motors, and we wore our hands raw with frantic tugging. Once, far out on the lake, when the winds came rushing along the Continental Divide in which the lake was set like a glittering blue jewel, we pulled anchor, could not start the motor, and drifted half across the lake before another fisherman came after us. I tried to row, busted an oar, and ripped more skin off the palms of my hands.

On the fourth morning the alarm was only a dull ringing far

back in my head. The ringing stopped and then the memory of it woke me. I went into his room to wake him, but he only turned and arched up his body like a cat stretching. "I can't . . ." he said. "I can't make it today."

I dressed and gathered up my fly rod and the little teardrop net I always wore fastened to my vest, and the burlap creel in which I carried my reels and flies. I went down to the lake alone, which is how I usually fished anyway. It was better alone, I thought. Then you didn't have to worry if the other person was enjoying himself, whether he would catch the fish you had dreamed of all winter, whether he would see your poor casts. Sometimes with the experts, I'd seen fishing turn to fierce competition.

The boy had stopped casting that last afternoon. I had asked him why, and he had answered curtly, "What's the use?"

"They're here," I told him. "Big ones. Up to four, five, even ten pounds."

"Sure," he said.

"They are. Dave told me he hooked a tremendous trout here last September. He had it on for nearly an hour. He said it was actually . . ."

"Towing his boat. You've told me that. In Cincinnati, Sioux City, Cody, and . . ."

"Guess I did," I said. "But they're here. I'll swear to it."

"Then why haven't we caught any?" he asked.

"Maybe they haven't come into the channel yet; maybe we haven't found the right fly or lure; maybe . . ."

"Maybe they're not here," he said. "Maybe they were here sixteen years ago, when you say you caught all those monsters."

"Yes, they were here," I said quietly. "I killed a great number of trout when I came to the lake sixteen years ago."

"You said your arms were tired from catching so many."

"They were."

"You said *my* arms would be tired."

I had looked out across the lake, at the surrounding sagebrush flat with its pastures and fences and scattered trees, and at the mountains of the Continental Divide that rimmed the lake, some still snowcapped though it was midsummer. We had fished seven hours without a strike, and the sun was now high and hot.

"Can't we go back," he said, "or run the boat around the lake a couple of times? I like to run the kicker."

The word sounded strange on his tongue. It was a new word and fit him like a readymade suit. We had not been in a boat together before, and I was pleased that he enjoyed running the kicker.

"I'd like to fish," I said.

"For how long?" he asked, turning from me and fingering the rubber covering on the handle of the kicker, turning it slightly several times without pulling the cord.

"We came a long way to fish this lake," I said. "More than two thousand miles. I think we'll get some trout if we'll . . . only . . . be patient enough."

"Well, I'm tired."

And then he put the rod in the bottom of the aluminum boat carelessly and tucked his head down into his mackinaw jacket though the sun was high and hot. I fished for another half hour and didn't catch a thing.

On the fourth morning the air was wet and cold. There was a thin drizzle and I rolled down the rim of the expensive khaki hat I'd bought in the city a week before the trip and lifted the collar of my old hunting coat. This time I pressed the rubber bulb near the gasoline can four or five times sharply before I pulled the cord, pumping it until it grew hard. The motor started on the first pull, and I backed out of the dock and out into the springs.

There were a few lights, and the moon still gave enough light to see by. I eased the boat under the wire that stretched across the springs into which the fish came when the weather warmed, and headed out into the channel. When I was parallel to the great clump of willows on shore, I turned left and cut my speed, running the boat slowly out until I thought I was in the deepest part of the channel; "Glory Hole" the spot was called—and I had only learned of it the day before, from the manager of the cabins. I had fished in the springs the first time I'd come to the lake; there had been thousands of trout in the springs and no need to fish from a boat. I had caught and killed a great number of them one night sixteen years earlier. It was better that the springs were closed, but I had hoped the boy could fish in them and catch some of the huge trout I had caught. One fish would be enough, if it was the right fish.

I let down the large tin can filled with cement. The anchor chain felt cold and harsh against my torn hands. The barest light was breaking behind the mountains to the east; it came first from the V of the mountains, where two pyramids crossed, and then the whole sky to the east grew lighter.

I tied on a long brown leech, with a brown marabou tail, wet it in my mouth, and then began to strip line from my new Princess reel. Soon I had a good length of line working back and forward, and then I laid it out as far as I could and dropped the rod tip to the surface of the water, as I'd seen several men do the day before. In a minute or so, I began the methodical short-strips' retrieve, slowly bringing the fly back through the black waters. It was a rhythmic process and not at all like the dry-fly fishing I had always done in the East. Everything was feel. I had fished the lake with spinning lures that summer after my release from the army; I had come alone and stayed for four days that had stayed pristine these past sixteen years. But now, with flies, I had not been able to induce a strike. Five, six times I cast, and each time waited and then brought the fly back slowly—strip, strip, strip, pause; strip, strip, strip.

It was good, I thought, that the boy had not come out with me. The air grew colder as the mists formed on the lake and the drizzle grew into a light rain. My hands were already numb, and no one else had yet come out onto the lake. I heard unseen sheep bleating in one of the meadows.

I enjoyed being on the lake alone, and I enjoyed casting the long line and then bringing back the fly with that slow, methodical retrieve. The years had been long and crowded and hard, and I had watched some of my dreams die and I had not been home enough—not nearly enough—and I had thought all winter and all spring, for several years, of coming back to this lake, where I had once made such a large catch. I wanted to catch some of the big trout very much, on flies. You progressed from worms to lures to flies, and then flies made all the difference. I had wanted the boy to catch some of the big trout, it didn't matter how.

The tip of my rod jerked down sharply. I raised it and felt the heavy throbbing as the line arched out and away. It was a good fish.

The fish moved off to the left and I reeled in the loose line so I could fight him from the reel. Twice he broke water but did not jump. Cutthroat, I thought. I knew that the cutthroat broke water but that the brooks in this lake usually did not. There were hybrids in the lake, too, crosses between the rainbow and the cutthroat, but they would not often jump either.

The fish was not as large as I'd pictured him, and I soon had him alongside and into my little stream net. It was about two pounds, and since we wouldn't be eating them, I took the hook out and then turned out the net. In the net the fish was bright red; and I watched as he wavered slowly, his back spotted and the red no longer visible, and then darted down and out of sight.

I cast out immediately, and after waiting for the fly to sink, began the slow retrieve again. Again the rod tip shot down, and I took another cutthroat, about the same size. When I had turned this one out of the net, I sat down on the green boat cushion and took out a cigar. I breathed deeply several times, lit my cigar, and looked over toward the east. It was still raining lightly, and the sun had not yet broken. Christ, it was good to be out on this lake alone, after all the years, after all the changes.

Several other boats were anchored in the channel now, and a man in one of them was fast to a good fish.

"On the leech?" the other man called out.

"Yep. Brown and long, with marabou."

I waited another ten minutes, while the fish was brought in. As the man finally lifted it high with his huge boat net, I could see it was a gorgeous male brookie.

The other man had a fish on now, too. The trout had come into the hole. There might be hundreds of them, staging into the channel that led to the springs.

I cast again, and again took a fine trout. I was in the right spot, in the right hole, and there were many fish and I had the right fly.

I took two more, about three pounds each, and then, after three fruitless casts, hooked a fish I could not stop. I felt when he took that he was heavy. He did not rush like the others, angling to one side while the line angled up and up. This fish moved straight away from the boat—slowly and steadily. *Thump—thump— thump.* Soon he had all my stripping line out, and then began to take line off the reel with the same slow, confident power.

And then he stopped.

I lifted the rod tip to be sure it was still there. There was a heavy weight, but I felt no movement. Perhaps he was sulking, I thought. I lifted the rod again and felt the same dead weight. For several minutes I stood, putting constant pressure on the line but not enough to break it. My chest was beating heavily; my right hand shook.

"In the weeds?" one of the men asked.

"Don't know. Something's still down there. I can feel something."

"Better pull the line with your hand," the man said. "If he's still on, you'll feel him."

I did so and only felt the dead weight.

I gave the line a few more steady pulls, and then drew it tight and gave it a sharp tug. When I got the line in, I saw some weeds still attached to it. The fish had wound himself around and around until he was able to break off; I'd never felt the break.

"Tough luck," one of the men called. "Must have been a big brookie—or a hybrid."

"I couldn't turn him," I said.

"One of the big hybrids, probably. Eight, maybe ten pounds. Larger even."

I took a deep breath and sat down. My hands were still shaking so I pressed them against my knees. Then I went into my fly box and fumbled for another of the leeches I'd been given by a neighbor the day before. I breathed deeply again, thought of the boy, and decided to head back to the cabin.

"You really took five and lost a big one?" the boy said as we sat at the linoleum table. His eyes were wide and his bushy black hair, dried by the sun, stood up wildly. He was rested and I could tell he was excited as he wolfed down a doughnut we'd bought in town the night before. "Five? And they were about three pounds? Why didn't you keep them? I'd have kept them. Every one of them."

"All the men were getting good fish," I said.

"Why didn't you wake me?"

"I tried to, old man, but you wouldn't be woke."

"Want to go back out? Do you think I can get a couple? *Everyone was getting them?* How many fish did you actually see caught?"

"Whenever you're ready we'll go out," I said, smiling.

"You're sure I can get some? They're in the channel, like the manager said they'd be this week?"

"Let's find out," I said.

The lake was crowded now. As I moved the boat out of the springs and into the channel, I could see at once that the Glory Hole now had eight or ten boats anchored in or near it. The sun had burned off the mist and the rain had stopped; it was late morning, and I could see down into the water, right to the bottom in the areas that didn't have weeds. It was a shallow lake, and not particularly clear, and in the summer the weeds grew thick and high. I saw several large fish swimming slowly along the bottom and cut the motor. The boy looked over the side as we circled back, and he saw them too. They were large brook trout—four or five pounds apiece.

"Did you see them, Dad?" he asked. "Did you see the *size* of them?"

"I saw."

"Shall we fish here?"

"Let's head farther out," I said. "Near where I got them this morning."

We headed out toward the hole, but several boats were anchored where I had been. I did not want to fish too close to them. I wished there were no other boats on the lake.

Finally, we cut the motor at the edge of the weeds, where the hole abruptly ended. I told the boy to cast in toward the other boats. His rod was rigged, and he began to cast before I'd fully lowered the anchor chain. He drew the lure back quickly, with the rod tip held high and steady. He made four casts this way; I watched him while I tied on another leech and checked my leader for frays.

"Put the rod tip down and bring the lure back in short jerks," I said. "You're bringing it back too fast."

"Like this?" he asked, and lowered the rod and brought the lure back even faster, still without the short jerks that had worked so well for me sixteen years earlier.

"No, no," I said. "Slower. Slower."

One of the men in my morning spot had hooked another fish on a fly rod, and he fought it noisily, with Texas howls. The boy looked over and then began to reel his lure in fast again.

In a few minutes another man had a fish on his fly rod, and then another rod bent in that high curving arc, too. I began to cast now, from the bow of our boat, and on the third cast hooked a solid cutthroat.

"This spinning rod is no good," the boy said.

"It will catch more and bigger fish than a fly," I told him.

"That's what you said while we were driving here. All the way across the country you told me I'd have no trouble catching fish with a spinning rod. I haven't gotten a thing. Not a strike."

I put my rod down and took his spinning rod. It was a strange weapon in my hands. I had not used one in many years. I had stopped using a spinning rod after I'd fished this lake the last time, and I had gone through a long apprenticeship learning the magic of a fly rod. I had caught nothing for a long time, and then suddenly the line no longer whipped down on the water behind me, and the fly no longer slapped down on the water, and my distance grew from twenty to forty and then maybe sixty-five feet.

I flicked the metal lure far out into the hole and let it sink, and then brought it back in short, sharp jerks. I cast three or four more times, drew the lure back with those slow, sharp jerks, and then handed the rod to the boy. He cast again, and then again. He imparted a better motion to the lure now, but he still caught no fish. The other men took three more fish on their fly rods.

I cast again, and then again. On the fourth cast I hooked another cutthroat; he splashed at the surface several times, and then came in without difficulty.

"I can't get a thing," the boy said. "I'm just no good at it. I'll never catch anything."

"You will. I'm sure you will."

"You've been saying that."

"Try a few more casts," I coached.

"Why?"

"You can't catch anything if you don't cast."

The sun was bright and hot now, and many of the boats were beginning to head back to the dock. I pulled the anchor and headed closer to the center of the hole.

But when we'd anchored in the new spot and he'd cast four or five more times, he gave it up and sat down.

"How long are we going to stay here?" he asked.

"We can go back now," I said. "I only wanted you to get a couple of fish."

"I haven't caught any," he said.

"I know," I said.

"Look, Dad," he said. "I like fishing, I really do. And I like being out here with you. But I can't catch anything on this spinning rod. Maybe if I knew how to use a fly rod it would be different. But I don't. And I don't have the same kind of patience you have. I like fishing, but I don't like not catching anything. You don't care. You really don't. But I do. And I'm not going to get any. Not today. Not tomorrow. Not any day this week. I know I won't."

"Well," I said, scratching my head, "why don't you try twenty more casts, and if you don't get one we'll head back to the cabin and maybe visit Virginia City or the Park this afternoon." Perhaps we should head back at once, I thought. I had enjoyed being on the lake alone at daybreak—catching some fish, losing the big fish. Perhaps it had been a mistake to come back to this lake with the boy. He would have enjoyed the beach more, and I wouldn't have wanted to fish so much. I never seemed to fish enough but it mattered much less when there were no trout nearby.

The boy began casting and counting, bringing in the lure much too fast. Thirteen, fourteen, fifteen. Nothing. Sixteen. Nothing.

On the seventeenth cast, the little glass rod jerked down in a sharp arc. A good fish. A very good fish.

"Good grief!" he shouted. "Can't hold him!"

"Let him have line," I shouted back. "Don't force him. Keep your rod tip high. It's a good fish, a *very* good fish."

The fish moved steadily from the boat. I could tell by the way the line throbbed slowly that it was a substantial fish, a brookie I thought.

The boy lowered the rod tip and I leaned over to lift it up. The boat swayed and I never reached the rod, but the boy smiled broadly and raised the rod so that the full force of the bend could work against the fish.

Don't lose it. For godsake don't lose it, I thought.

"He's still taking line, Dad. I can't stop him."

"He'll turn," I said. "He's got to turn in a minute or two. Don't force him. Don't let him get into the weeds, but don't force him. *Don't drop that rod tip!*"

The line went slack.

"No. No!" I said.

"Have I lost him? No. I *can't* have lost him."

"Reel quickly," I said. "Maybe he's turned. Maybe he's still there."

"He's there," the boy shouted. "I can feel him. Good grief, he's big. Can you see him yet? I won't lose him now."

I looked over where the line entered the water. I strained to see the fish, but could not. It had to be a big brookie.

Now the fish was angling off to the left. He might go completely around the boat. As the line came toward me, I lifted it and let it pass over my head: for a second I could feel the big fish throbbing at the other end of the line. The fish came around the front of the boat and the boy fought him on the other side.

We both saw it at the same time. A huge male brookie. We saw it twisting and shaking ten feet below the surface, the silver lure snug in the corner of its mouth.

"It's huge. It's the biggest brookie I've ever seen."

"I'm not going to lose him," the boy said. "I can't lose it now."

"You won't lose it. He's well hooked. He's too high and too tired to get into the weeds. You've got him beat, son. I'll get the net." I looked down under the seat and came up with the little teardrop stream net.

"He'll never fit," the boy said. "He'll *never* fit in that—*whooooa*. He's taking line again. He's going around the other side of the boat now."

The fish was close to the boat but not yet beaten. He went deep and around the corner of the boat. I watched for the line to angle out, on the other side of the boat. It never did.

"The anchor chain!" I shouted. "Don't let him get in the anchor chain."

"I can't feel him," said the boy. "The line's on something but I can't feel the fish fighting anymore."

I scurried the length of the boat, bent under the rod, and then lowered myself where the anchor chain entered the water. At first I could see nothing. But then I saw it. The huge brook trout was still on the line; I could see it five feet down, the silver lure still in the corner of its mouth. He was circling slowly around the anchor chain, and I could see that the line was already wound six or seven times around the links. It would not come free. Not ever.

"Is it there?" the boy called. "Is it still there?"

"You're going to lose him, son. He's in the anchor chain. There's no way I can get it free."

"Oh, no, no," he said.

I put my nose down to the surface of the water. The fish had gone around the chain twice more, and his distance from the chain was growing smaller and smaller. It kept circling, slowly, every now and then jerking its head back against the tug of the line.

"I can't lose him! I can't," the boy said.

"There's nothing to be done. If I lift the chain, he'll break off; if I leave him, he'll pull out in another couple of turns."

"What about the net."

"Don't think I can reach him."

"Try, Dad. Please try. I can't lose this fish. Not this one."

I took the little stream net and dipped it far down. The cold water stung my raw hands, and the net came short by more than a foot. The fish made a lunge and I was sure it would break free.

"Got him?"

"Nope. Too far down. Can't reach him."

"Maybe someone with one of the boat nets . . ." But he stopped. The other boats were gone from the lake; we had the Glory Hole to ourselves.

The fish went around the rope again. There was only a foot and a half between him and the chain now. The big brookie was tired. It was half on its side.

I took the boy's arm and pulled him down to where I knelt. It didn't matter if he let the line go slack now. Together we pushed our faces close to the surface of the water and peered down. In the liquid below us, we looked through the reflections of both our faces, side by side, overlapping and rippled, and saw the huge fish.

I reached again, pressing the net down through the water as carefully as I could, trying hard not to frighten it again. My arm was in up to my shoulder and I felt the cold lake water slosh onto my chest. The fish came a little higher this time. I could almost touch it with the end of the net—and I saw clearly now that even if I could get near enough to it, the fish was far too big for the little net, and the lure was almost torn out. There was no chance.

"You'll never get him, Dad," the boy said.

He was holding onto my shoulder now with his left arm, and looking constantly through our reflections at the shadow that was his fish.

"It's lost," I whispered.

And then the fish floated up five or six inches, I pressed the net toward its head, felt cold water on my face, saw the head of the huge fish go into the net, saw the line break behind the lure, and lifted madly.

A year has passed, and the etching remains, as if fixed by acid in steelplate: our faces in the water, merged; the tremendous circling trout; the fish half in and half out of that tiny teardrop net, and then the two of us, side by side in the bottom of that aluminum boat, our raw hands clutching a thing bright silver grey and mottled, and laughing as if we were four days drunk.

11

A Tale of
Two Fishes

I HAD RATHER GOTTEN OUT OF THE HABit of vacationing. For seven years, bucking the New York current, I'd held two full-time jobs and more, and with four young children and no car we traveled little and never for more than a day or two at a time. I had to borrow time from each job to meet special commitments at the other, and if I managed to take two weeks a year it was always in dribs and drabs.

But in early August, abruptly, without warning, there opened before us a full week—with two weekends—and it seemed just this side of heaven. The children were in summer camp, and Mari and I looked at each other with newlywed wonder. A whole week!

Naturally I decided we should go to the Battenkill. There was a huge dusk hatch of mayflies in early August, and the trout rose freely from eight thirty until midnight. "We'll stay at a motel right on the river," I told her as we sat at the dining room table, scheming, "and I'll fish every evening."

"*Every* evening?" she asked quietly.

"Unless it rains."

"Sounds like fun."

"I'm mad to catch that dusk hatch. They're big cream mayflies, size ten or twelve, and when they come off the water the fish . . ."

"I'm sure it will be wonderful for you." She lowered her head. "Couldn't we perhaps spend a few days, just two or three days of the vacation on Martha's Vineyard? I'd love to swim and sunbathe and paint; I hear it's absolutely breathtaking."

Martha's Vineyard was not one of our household words. I waited for the pitch—obviously planned and timed—to continue.

"Edna St. Vincent Millay raved about it," she said. "And it's romantic and windswept. Oh, Nick, wouldn't it be wonderful to swim in the ocean before breakfast and lie out in the sun all day and walk along the beach at night? You really need a rest, you know, and there's no place like the shore for a real rest. You can sleep all day in the sun, with the surf pounding in your ears, and swim . . ."

"They have a pool at the motel," I said quietly. "And I don't even know where Martha's Vineyard is."

"We'll get a map."

"It might take three days to get there; there could be all sorts of complications. You mean you don't even know where it is?"

"It's in New England, isn't it? An island, I think. And the Beaverhead or Bottomkill or what's-its-name is in New England, isn't it?"

Yes, the Battenkill was indeed in New England, I admitted, and thought that, alas, if *I* hadn't had a vacation in seven years, neither had Mari. "All right," I said, with magnanimous condescension and the wisdom of Solomon, "we'll split it in two: five days on the Battenkill, three on Martha's Vineyard."

"Four," she said.

"Three. Not a day more."

We rented a car on Saturday morning and, without reservations, found a good motel with a pool not far from Manchester. It was directly on the highway and cars rushed past constantly. But the rooms were comfortable, when you were in the pool you could almost forget there were a dozen people sitting on chairs around the perimeter and cars rushing by a couple a minute, and it wasn't far from the Battenkill, and they took Magi-Card.

I had the river much to myself and fished a stretch above Shushan, New York, that in May was more crowded than a rush-hour subway. At dusk, when the stream grew still, the large cream mayflies began to come off the water—two, three, and then the water was pocketed with rising trout and the air full of fluttering duns. Swallows began to dip and dart, to hover in the air and catch the rising mayflies. Even when I couldn't see the flies anymore, I could hear and see the birds working, all up and down the river.

I stood in the hushed alley of the Battenkill, gaining back some of myself, some of that which the city had sorely threatened, and caught four or five modest brown trout on Cream Variants, just at and after dusk, and then released them. It would have been enough without the fish—only to be standing alone in the river at that hour, feeling the bamboo of my delicate Dickerson fly rod come alive and work out the line with measured rhythms. But there was more: I missed a fish that first night which was extremely large. I'd failed to change to a heavier leader after dark, and the fish took in a splashy rise and snapped off almost at once.

Mari had not wanted to remain alone at the motel, and when I came off the river, about ten thirty, she was curled miserably into the corner of the car, half-asleep, half-starved, bitten to shreds by no-see-ums and mosquitoes. She was such a mess that, as I rushed her back to the motel, in a rash moment, I promised her *four* days on Martha's Vineyard.

Several days later I realized quite how rash I'd been. The fish I'd lost was indeed huge. I hooked him again the next night, and that time he jumped twice—high and thunderously—and then summarily headed downstream and broke me off in the dark. He was a full twenty inches, a superb old Battenkill brown, and a fever to land him raced through me. The next night, fishing the same run, I caught two good fish, but could not raise the big one. Battenkill browns strike hard after dark; the alley of the river is all hushed and misty and you can barely see the fly as it comes downstream toward and past you. The fish took like bass, crashing up, exploding the water and often jumping immediately after feeling the hook. Each time I thought I had the big one again.

On my last night I saw the huge brown rising steadily far beneath a wide batch of overhanging willow branches on the far bank. He began to come up for the mayflies just at dusk, and then stayed fixed in that position under the willows, his body a long shadow and his fin and tail partially above the surface. I knew I'd have trouble casting to him; the fly would have to be presented upstream of the branches, and then floated down under them. The angle was difficult and I knew the fly would drag uninvitingly. I tried a dozen casts and each time knew the fly was dragging badly by the time it reached the huge fish. The only way to take him, I finally reasoned, was to cross the stream to a spot directly above him, and then fish directly downstream with a lot of slack line. It is extremely difficult to wade any river after dark, and sections of the Battenkill, with its deceptive current and smooth stones, are especially hazardous. I inched my way upstream, with a kind of shuffling movement. The air was now quite cool and it had begun to drizzle. Thirty feet above the willow, I began to work my way slowly across stream. I took three small steps, tripped, held on tight to my precious Dickerson, and then went down on one knee in the river. The cold water shot into my waders, I regained my balance, and I knew I was done for the night.

No matter, I thought, as I headed back to the motel: I'll raise him tomorrow.

Mari smiled broadly when I came in, drenched and shivering. She had already packed our few valises, and wondered whether we couldn't leave right then, after I changed, for Martha's Vineyard. I knew I could take that huge brown the next evening; I knew he'd been there, and I knew how to raise him. I'd use a sturdy 3X leader, take up my position *above* him while it was still light, and then . . .''

"Why *don't* we leave now?" asked Mari. "It's probably not more than a few hours."

I was about to ask her, plead to her, if we couldn't stay over one more evening; I desperately wanted one more try at that fish. But I saw it was no use. "All right," I said. "But not tonight. We've never even located the place on the map."

"We always do it that way, don't we? We live with our heads in concrete all year long, and it's sort of like pioneering to head out and not know precisely where you're going."

"The great adventurers," I said.

It took us about seven hours of dull driving to reach Woods Hole, which a good guidebook proclaimed was the gateway to the Vineyard. It was an excruciatingly hot day, and the traffic on Route 7 was heavy; we fell behind some slow-moving trucks and crawled out of Vermont and down through Massachusetts. We breezed along the Massachusetts Turnpike and my only worry, after several hours, was that I'd spent half my vacation on the road.

We got to Woods Hole about 3:45 and were directed onto a long line of cars. A few discreet inquiries made me realize we should have made reservations in advance—years in advance—but I trotted over to the ticket office and thought myself lucky to get signed on (one-way only, since the Steamship Authority was booked solid for all return trips through Labor Day). I took the opportunity to note that I had only about $35 left in cash; Magi-Card had proved its worth—would it hold up for three days on an unknown island? We managed to become the last car wedged—brilliantly, I thought—onto the ferry, and as the boat and dock diverged it occurred to me, fleetingly, that if all return trips were booked through Labor Day, we might not get back to New York for a month. Which my publishing house might not appreciate.

I mentioned this to Mari, but she considered it too sober an issue to consider at such an exciting time. We had three days to worry about that, didn't we? Anyway, she was too busy watching some of the initiates feed popcorn to the trailing gulls, letting the kernels sweep back until one of the poised birds caught it in midair.

We got to the island about six. Vineyard Haven was crowded, and we'd seen its likes before, so we drove to Oak

Bluffs, which was about the same. We saw a few motels here and there, and a number of inns, but none of them displayed the prominent golden-orange Magi-Card sign.

"Why don't we explore the island before we eat and find a place to stay?" said Mari. "Maybe there are sections that aren't so crowded." This was a fatal suggestion.

The New England guidebook's map of Martha's Vineyard showed us where we were and suggested that up-island, near Menemsha, Chilmark, and Gay Head, we'd find the quiet we were seeking. It was nearly seven now, and we both rather could have eaten dinner; but we decided that the island was small enough for a quick tour, and maybe we'd find something pleasant and isolated at the other end.

We drove for more than a half hour, looking at the small farms and weatherworn saltbox houses, the ponds and salt marshes. Finally, driving slowly through a nest of unmarked roads, I saw a small sign that read LOBSTERVILLE BEACH. We hadn't seen the ocean yet, so I took the road.

It was a lovely beach, strewn with small pebbles and curving in a wide arc. The sun was half-down now, and the clouds were richly maroon. I took Mari's hand and we walked up over a bluff together and stood quietly, looking out over the lakelike cove. It was rather a holy moment. There wasn't an evening hatch to worry about, not even a twenty-inch brown trout, and I sort of began to think that friendship with one's wife was almost as pleasant as trout fishing.

We held hands for a full five minutes and spoke softly, as married people sometimes do, about bringing some canvas down the next day, for Mari to paint, and collecting some of the brightly colored rocks, and of how much the children would love a beach like this. It had been, by now, a long, hot, tiring day—a full twelve hours since we'd left Manchester. I flexed my aching shoulders back, snapped a small crick out of my neck, and asked Mari if she was hungry.

"Hmm, yes," she said, "but it's so-oo beautiful here, isn't it? So absolutely quiet and still. The skies are unbelievable. You couldn't paint them. No one would believe those colors. The ocher bluffs up there on the left, the little town way off there; the way the sky is divided into shifting planes of maroon and crimson and Payne's grey; the way those birds are cutting the stillness of the background. See how excited they are.''

"Birds?" I asked.

"Over there." She pointed to the left and I saw a great flock of terns dipping and swooping. Something was agitating the surface, too, and as the birds came closer I could hear their shrill, excited calls.

"What is it?" asked Mari. "Is it a raise?"

"Rise," I said absently. "Yes, rise. No. But they're after something. Minnows. Killies. I don't know what you call them. Small fish of some kind. Not much." I looked more carefully. The water beneath the screaming birds, only a few hundred yards from us now, was tremendously choppy. I saw several sharp splashes, and then the silver blue back of fish—two, four, a dozen very large fish. But the area was a hundred yards long—and it was all choppy and agitated. Bluefish. A huge school of blues had trapped baitfish and were on a massive feed; the birds were picking up the piccos. I'd read about blues and I'd caught a few, on a party boat out of Sheepshead Bay, deep and on heavy lines, when I was young. They're a ferocious fish—powerful and savage. I'd never seen them working like this—and the action was coming directly toward us, and now not more than fifteen or even ten feet from shore in some places.

I could feel my heart beginning to pound heavily. Mari said something but I didn't hear her. Several wild men came racehorsing up the beach with huge spinning rods and cast long plugs far out and then jerked them back quickly, quicker than I'd ever seen a plug worked, across the surface. In less than a minute, both rods were bent in sharp arcs and the reels were whirring as line raced out; they were hooked up to heavy fish. The birds were directly over our heads now, and the chopping water directly in front of me. I took my cigar out of my mouth and flipped it like an immie, as far as I could. It disappeared in a massive swirl.

"Where are you going?" shouted Mari.

I didn't answer. I chewed up the beach toward the car, unlocked the luggage compartment, and began to take my bamboo rod out of its aluminium case. My whole body was shaking uncontrollably now. I soon had my Dickerson jointed, and was about to fit on the Hardy reel when the men came rushing up the bluff, leaped into Jeeps, and roared off around the cove. I trotted to the top of the bluff, rod and reel in my hands, and looked for birds. There were none.

"Mari," I shouted. "Let's go."

When she came up, somewhat slowly, I rather roughly hustled her into the car. "Good thing," I said excitedly, "I didn't get the Dickerson set up in time. Damned good thing. Did you see those monsters? Eight, ten pounders. No less. They'd eat twenty-inch trout, wouldn't they? Good thing I restrained myself: I'd still be picking slivers of my Dickerson out of the sand."

"Beginning to like Martha's Vineyard?" Mari asked.

"There are the birds again," I said. "Over there." And I began racing along the narrow macadam road. A mile down the road and the birds seemed to be hanging in the air directly to my left. So I ran the car high up into a sand dune where it would be safely off the road, leaped out, and raced to the top of a nearby dune.

The birds were too high; they were only circling; the fish had either gone down deep or moved out. I breathed heavily and walked back to the car where Mari was sadly shaking her head and smiling.

"Gone," I said.

"Good," she said.

"Let's go eat," I said.

"And find a place to sleep," she said.

We were both starved and tired; the sun was low and the air had begun to grow cool. I started the motor, switched into reverse, and stepped on the gas. The car wiggled back, the tires spun, and I thought we sank a bit lower.

"Ha!" I said.

"Stuck?" she said.

"Have to do this slowly," I said, and began to push down lightly on the gas pedal. The car wiggled, the tires spun, and again I thought we sank a bit lower.

"Slowly?" she said.

"Maybe it's fast," I said, and gunned the motor hard. This time there was no doubt at all about the issue: we sank so deep into the soft sand I could hardly open the door to get out and begin my shoveling, with a weathered board, riveted with nails, I found nearby.

I dug for twenty minutes, furiously, but the car only seemed to sink lower. "Hopeless," I said. "We'll be here for a month." We were at the end of the island, with no houses nearby, with only the faint outline of a town off to the right. I decided to head for the town.

It was nearly dark now, so I trotted away at a brisk clip and found that on this magical island, beloved by Edna St. Vincent Millay and my wife, the towns receded. This one did, or seemed to. It even did more. I chugged up a little hill and, looking down, discovered that it had disengaged itself from the land I was standing on: it was actually on the other side of a moat—or maybe an inlet. So I walked back slowly, barely able to face my good wife, who had suffered once again such humiliation and privation at the hands of a fanatic fisherman.

But Mari was almost cheery when I returned—and the car was out of the sand.

"Pushed it," she said.

"Like hell!"

I got in and started the motor. "At least I didn't use my Dickerson on those monsters," I said. I put the car in forward gear and almost leaped into the sand trap again.

"Fish!" muttered Mari. "At least the fishermen who pulled me out know enough to come in Jeeps."

I didn't say a word until we got to Edgartown and Mari wanted to stop at the first lodging place we passed. Then I reminded her that we had to live on Magi-Card alone, and we drove slowly and intently in and out of the narrow one-way streets until finally, like palm trees in the desert, a golden orange sign sprang up in the window of the Harborside Inn.

It was cheap at any price, and soon we were changed and

washed and eating huge platters of roast beef. We even drank cool wine and danced a middle-aged fox-trot—something we hadn't done for years—in the Navigator Room. It cost only a signature.

The next day I rented myself a saltwater spinning rod and caught bluefish until I couldn't move my arms—also my first striped bass, about twelve pounds, on a surface plug, and fell in love with that grand fish for life.

Mari found herself some sun and some rocks, some beautiful views and some quiet sandy beaches. We swam and we walked hand in hand for miles, barefoot, along the north shore, filling a fish creel with brightly colored stones and shells. We walked along the road, too, barefoot and content at dusk, beside the Bouncing Bet and the blue-petaled chicory, listening to the long sweet songs of the cicadas. And at night we walked through the narrow streets of Edgartown and looked in galleries and shopwindows and ate more roast beef and lobster, and danced close. I fished only that first day, intently, in the brightest sun, without a hat or shirt.

We had to return on Sunday, and so did a couple thousand other people. Obviously they all couldn't get into that ferry—and at this time we learned about the standby system. We stood by and stood by from eight that morning until ten thirty that night, when they put on an extra boat. About three that afternoon, when we were nearly roast beef from the heat, I saw John Updike blithely drive up, get on line, push his sunglasses up on his forehead, and move on board within fifteen minutes.

"Place is loaded with famous writers," I told Mari.

"Who plan ahead," she said.

We got back to New York at five thirty in the morning, with seventy-three cents between us, too tired to take more than essential luggage from the car. The next morning, before racing to the subway, I noticed that the car had been broken into and all our shells stolen. No matter. I still had my brutal sunburn, an epic rash of poison ivy on both legs, and a wallet full of Magi-Card receipts.

But it wasn't so bad, I thought, as I pleasantly elbowed an old lady who'd elbowed me on the sunburn in the jammed subway: maybe I won't be able to vacation again for another seven years.

12

Big Muddy

ON OPENING DAYS WHEN HUNCHED, overdressed men cluster in groups along the frozen banks and stamp their feet like dray horses in winter, for warmth, Big Muddy fiercely resists the siege. Unruly, off-color, and bloated, its waters rise to the challenge of defending its denizens against their worst assault. But fish have been put in and fish are extracted—pale, silvery fish that flip and flap a few times and then capitulate.

Some of the river is not impossible to fish during the early weeks, but most of it is. In certain accessible deep pools and eddies, a night crawler or live minnow will tempt those hatchery trout that can be reached; and I have seen them caught beneath the large stone dam and along certain banks at bends where the river runs heavy and slow. But most of the stream I call Big Muddy racehorses along at such a disquieting gallop, and has such a cof-

fee-with-milk color, that even most of the hatchery trout are unavailable, thank you.

The river runs high in the early spring, completely covering
the innumerable boulders in the four-mile run of the lower river
below the dam. Even spinners are no use here, for the gradient is
sharp and the speed of the water too great: fish across or downstream and your lure sweeps to the top at once, yards from your
quarry; fish upstream at any angle and your lure must either hang
up on the boulders or speed downstream high above even the most
unwary stocked brookies. The tail ends of large rocks, completely
submerged, and behind which the trout surely take their cover,
simply cannot be fished to with lures. Nor can one get bait down
to the fish behind these boulders.

The river rises from three different sources in the mountains
and runs through miles of soft-sod cow pastures; in the early spring
the debris-flecked snow runoff, itself enough to put all fish down,
is matched by tons of soft earth sprung loose by the torrents. Still,
the river is fished most heavily during the early weeks—and
pressure on it is as severe as that on any stream within a similar
eighty miles of any major metropolis: fishermen cheek to jowl,
fishing bait and spinners; a fish is caught here and a fish there,
but few fishermen, for all their pounding and waiting, do much
better; the traditional Opening Day newsphoto of a beaming
angler with his limit of hatchery trout strung by the jaws along a
stick will be taken elsewhere.

Big Muddy has no lake or reservoir to feed it with spring-run
browns or rainbows—like the Esopus or Catherine Creek. Whatever it holds is soon and then thereafter fully its own: stockers that
have earned their right to stay, holdover browns of fourteen
inches or more, and browns born to the river. Though brook trout
are planted regularly each April, most are quickly harvested: I
have never seen one that had survived a season. The river is a
brown-trout river, muddy and complex.

Nor does Big Muddy receive any aid from conservationists,
who might plant willow shoots, build dams, restrict creel limits; it
is not a rated or blue-ribbon or legendary river, and its fans and
protectors are few. Fortunately the road builders have not yet

crossed its paths, and its own sweet misshapen and chameleon form goes unmolested by man, changed only by storms and severe winters and the laws of a stream highly vulnerable to natural change; from one year to the next, it differs radically—with new channels, new sandbars, even holding pools with new contours. The river reacts dramatically to the elements—and when it returns it is different. I have seen the little Green River in the Berkshires take ten hours of torrential rain and then become crystal green in three hours; I have heard that the Letort and other limestoners keep their level and clarity and form under the most trying provocations from nature. Big Muddy takes a week, two weeks, to clear its head and gather back its own, to collect and shrink itself back to itself, and by that time it's usually rained again. The river always comes back in a slightly different form: you cannot learn it all, not ever.

If rivers are like women, Big Muddy is ostensibly a bloated whore; but it has private lives, outside the trade.

Do not demean it because of its wantonness, its vulnerability. The high and muddy water, the constant change, preserves Big Muddy. Both its fish and its reputation are protected by these phenomena. Now and again, while speaking of the Beaverkill, the Battenkill, the Schoharie, I'll mention Big Muddy. Sheepishly. Without fail a nose turns up, lips curl. "Fished out." "Impossible to fish." "Pounded to death years ago." "They dump in a couple of thousand hatchery trout and they're gone in three weeks." "Who'd *want* to fish that muddy ditch, anyway?"

Fine. Wonderful.

The rivers I love best often have bad reputations.

I am delighted to hear such superior comments. They are a preserving music. I smile approval. They may have their sneers along with their Miramachi and their Madison; no doubt I could easily grow to love their rivers had I the time and money; I have grown easily to love a dozen others, as I could never love Big Muddy: the clear glides of the upper Beaverkill, the deep, sensuous pools of the Battenkill, the potholes of the Au Sable, with their rainbows sweeping up from boiling depths for a hair fly. It is easy enough to be romantically attached to those. Though I do not sneer at Big Muddy, I welcome every other man's sneer.

I never fished the river out of love in my early years, but because it was accessible. I had to make it do. And it has. When the streams sixty miles from the city became too dense with brother anglers, I hitchhiked the extra twenty miles to Big Muddy. Now it is as crowded as they were, and the trip that once took me three hours takes but one-and-a-half; but whereas they have become mere put-and-take propositions, the fishing today in Big Muddy is better than it ever was. For me at least. For I am a bit more privy to its secrets, an incurable sentimentalist about childhood friends, and most anglers have become lazy—preferring easier rivers, more highly rated rivers, even less well known rivers. Let them skirt the remote, untouched corners of Canada; it helps Big Muddy, and I still find enough in its muddy reaches to fatten my winter dreams.

I did not fish flies until I was out of my teens, so I learned Big Muddy on worms and spinners. If I had been too wanton on easier rivers, Big Muddy was my first lesson in humility: except for a few days when by chance I must have followed a hatchery truck by hours, and could horse out a limit in an hour, I never took trout there without hard work—without learning important lessons. It has become for me an example of what even the most uninviting and uninspiring rivers may contain—and its hard-won truths have served me well along the banks of its betters, with better gear and more delicate tactics.

Though Big Muddy is no secret stream, is available to all, it yet has its mysteries. I am just as pleased few know, for instance, that the river drops a full ten to twelve feet in many places after the spring runoff ceases; I am tickled few realize that the four-pounder someone took on a night crawler from below the dam was not a freak or a hatchery breeder. There are probably half a hundred such fish in its more than twelve miles of twisting water—and hundreds that have held over two and three years. I would as soon few realized the stream also produces its own fish; I have found the spawning beds in the fall, I have seen and caught the five- and six-inch browns, and I have caught enough brightly colored two- and three-year-old fish that I will swear were native to the river.

But if they did find out—not as I did, by tramping its banks for twenty years, but by tale or report—I should still not be too worried that my secret was threatened. They would not believe my stories, surely, but if they did I would have to tell them that most of the fish could not be caught, not readily, for Big Muddy fiercely protects its own.

Oh, the fish can be taken—some of them, even the largest of them, at certain times: but not all of them, not ever. At the right moment, which may or may not come in a given year, and at the right place, which will change each year, the largest of the browns —heavy fish with tough skins, bright markings, and mangled hooks for lower jaws—may show themselves and perhaps be taken.

Walk back from the road a mile or more along the heavily shrubbed and tangled banks of the upper river, up sharp shale and pebble hills that dissolve when your feet dig into them; crawl under masses of old and rusted barbed wire, and along sheer drops where the river is ten feet to the banks; take an hour, two hours, from your precious fishing time to explore back from that obvious couple of miles of unprotected water that everyone and his buddy fishes—and you will discover part of the reason there will always be fish in Big Muddy. There is nothing idyllic about the stream here, but you will see no forked sticks in the ground, no cardboard bait containers, no well-boot-marked banks. Not many anglers are foolhardy enough to tramp back into this unpromising wilderness.

And why would they?

See how inhospitable the water is—trees broken across the pools, their branches fingering out in a couple of dozen directions; potholes fifteen feet deep, with no way to fish a fly or lure in them; and that same off-color water, increased by the silt bottom and the cow pastures upstream. Make that trip once at the wrong time, perhaps in a rainstorm, as I've done, and not move or see a fish; sink to your hips in the soft-mud bottom; tear your net and your Hodgman's and your best fishing jacket; spend twenty minutes finding that one clear corner of a pool from which you can cast—

and then hang your lure up on the one branch you did not figure on beneath the surface: and I doubt if you will try it again soon— even if I were so foolhardy as to insist it would be worth your while.

Even if I were, and you believed me, wouldn't you admit: "It's not my brand of fishing, thank you!"

And that, perhaps is what most protects the upper Big Muddy. It is not, even when its secrets are revealed, a river most men would enjoy fishing. It is the kind of river a shrewd and tenacious local boy might learn to understand and respect—if fishing was his abiding love. But no one could ever love Big Muddy, like Marinaro his Letort, Flick his Schoharie, Darbee his East Branch: it is never beautiful or evocative; it has no clear glides and attractive riffles; it has no major hatches and few even worth classifying; and it is not even fertile. You might fish the upper river for a week without moving a trout—the best of you. Big Muddy's ways are maverick, undependable, frustrating. It is a tough, gnarled, unyielding, and inhospitable river. It demands men who can find pleasures astream on many fishless days.

There is a photograph taken by Vincent Marinaro of a six-pound native brown rising to a grasshopper on the Letort. The huge fish is caught at the split second it approaches within inches of the terrestrial on the surface; the jaws are already opening wide, the broad tail is curved as it angles up. It is an awesome photograph—dramatic, evocative, still. But when I view it, I think of something even more dramatic and telling: the man who crouched silently at his blind on an exquisite river for hours, at the precise place he knew the huge fish would be, waiting for the precise moment—and who then pounced like a panther with his camera.

Big Muddy is light years from the Letort; and I am even further from Marinaro. I also do not carry a camera. But I have waited, silently, a score of hours by those deep and opaque pools in the upper river; I have tossed worms and grasshoppers upstream and watched them drift down and out of sight. I have been there in the early mornings and at dusk: not fishing, just watching. I have never seen one of the large browns rise to the surface or, indeed, make any move to take such free-floating baits. I imagine them lying down below the main current, in the deepest hollowed-out lies, taking all their food from the floor of the river, or from what the low eddies swing to them. They are not only out of all sight, but protected by a maddening complex of currents and snags, in isolated pockets of safety. To hold the current, you would need a full ounce sinker; you would need twelve-pound test line; you would have to go straight down to them, through the tangled branches, with pinpoint drops from a fourteen-foot pole deftly extended. And still you would miss most of the lies most of the time. When I was a youngster I would have tried them that way, had I thought of it; and I may try them that way yet: for I do not want, ever—for all the fly-fishers' clubs I ever join and swear by—to advance too far from the pleasures and cunning of childhood. But for all practical purposes, they cannot be fished to for ninety-nine out of a hundred days of the season, with either flies or lures—and perhaps even with bait. There must be fifty such pockets of safety unavailable by any means, except when the river is at a particular level. Then how can I be so sure the big browns are there?

It is of course logical that they be there.

The stream is heavily stocked both above and below this back section of the upper river; though there are few important mayfly hatches, the river is rich in baitfish, hellgrammites, crawfish, and a vast array of bottom food; large numbers of worms are washed down from the cow pastures. If the water is uninviting to fishermen, it is obviously highly attractive to trout: and, safe in their stream coverts, with a substantial food supply and a limited number of competitors, the fish must obviously grow to large size.

I have more palpable proof.

One chill and drizzly Opening Day ten years ago, when I was out more for the ritual of tramping the banks and beginning a new season than with much expectation of moving a fish, I had worked my way far from the crowds, far up along the upper river. The nights had been well below freezing, and though snow was still heavy the water was clearer than I'd ever seen it—even in a dry fall. There was no snow runoff (the pastures were frozen solid), and the water was translucent and quite low.

I was fishing an oversized silver spinner across and downstream—letting it turn with the current, then flicking the reel handle backward so the lure could drop, flutter, and then rise before I brought it back ten feet, repeated the process with short jerks and then retrieved and cast again. I had neither touched nor seen a fish in three hours of hard fishing and knew that only the lower river, near the dam, had been stocked because of the heavy snow. Though the lower and uppermost stretches were crammed with fishermen, I had seen no other angler for several hours.

As noon approached, the sun appeared briefly and the snow began to glisten and run in places. I was working the fast rip at the head of a large holding pool, a pool heavily protected by fallen trees and innumerable outstretched branches both above and below the surface, when a large fish suddenly turned on my lure.

I did not feel him, and I doubted if he had felt the lure; but he had swirled and turned, his broad back well out of the water, right near the spinner. It was a slow, heavy turn and roll, when the spinner was inches below the surface—like that of a huge Hudson River carp, perhaps, or of a confident pike in midsummer. The depth of the rip was a full ten feet, I knew, so the fish most probably could not have been bottom feeding as I'd expected for this season, but roaming or lying in at least midwater, or higher.

I cast across and downstream again, and the boiling rip sped the lure into the heaviest current and to the surface. I turned the reel handle back three or four times, then stopped and gave several short jerks. The fish struck hard, felt the steel, and lurched off with the current smack into the pool below me.

He took perhaps thirty yards of line in a steady rush before I felt him slow. I was resigned that he would be lost in the maze of branches protecting the pool, but I pumped him gently and finally he turned back into the rip and worked upstream. Several times he headed back into the depths of the pool, but I gained line and the current began to tire him. It might have been a big smallmouth or a foul-hooked carp or sucker, for there are such in Big Muddy. He never jumped.

After a full half hour, I had him close and could see the sleek form, the heavily spotted back. I had no net, so I waited until he was fully exhausted and then beached him carefully on a little bar.

The fish went twenty-one inches. I killed it and examined the contents of its stomach. There were a score of nearly digested hellgrammite sections and nymphs, three undigested minnows, one brown trout four inches long, two night crawlers, and some ten or twelve colored pebbles.

I am quite sure that at that moment I could have raised him on a large nymph or perhaps any large fly fished across and down-stream—for the lure had been no more than inches beneath the surface and he had taken it readily. I have several times regretted that I did not hook him on a fly, for the outcome would have been much more in doubt: I doubt I could have held him.

What brought him up?

I can only think that this was one of those rare times when he had left the security of the deep hole and was lying in the rip, wantonly taking anything that came down. I presume he wintered and summered and remained always in the big pool, except for those infrequent moments when he moved into the rip to take stunned minnows or other bait caught in the heavy flow. He couldn't have seen them had the water been its usual muddy color; he probably would not have ventured up in crystal water, except at night. But for an hour, perhaps, while the water was turning, he had moved in securely for a heavy feed.

And I had been there.

I have fished that section and several others like it on Big Muddy several dozen times since then and only once moved another comparable fish. It was an old hook-jawed brown of more than five pounds, the largest I've ever taken in the East, its lower jaw a huge bent wart from grubbing along the bottom; the bump reminded me of the writing wart on Thomas Wolfe's middle finger. Though this was several weeks later in the season, the conditions were the same—clear water just beginning to turn.

In the summer and fall, I think perhaps these old cannibals move out of the holes at night to feed—but rarely otherwise. Why should they? And it is impossible to fish back in those tangles at night.

I have never caught or seen a fish under thirteen inches in these back sections. Stocking takes place three miles upstream and several miles below; if any hatchery trout work their way up or down into the mazes, it must be after they are able to fend for themselves, after they are already of some size: otherwise, they are no doubt frightened off, forced out because they cannot compete for food, or are even eaten by the big browns. And when, infrequently, one of the cannibals is taken, another good fish probably moves into the ideally protected lies, claims it for his own, and then grows equally fat and fierce and cunning. The infrequent angler who may explore back into the upper river will be discouraged as much by the lack of action as by the difficulty of the trip. For myself, knowing the big trout are there makes all the difference.

When I go with a friend, I like to have him drop me off at the town bridge while he drives several miles upstream. I like to work my way slowly through the entire three-mile run and then meet him four or five hours later. The footprints disappear after the first quarter mile, and I have the shrub tangles, the cliffs and the deep pools to myself. Each time I make the trip I discover a new holding pool; each time there are new fishable rips and runs.

The stream has as little consistency as any woman I ever met.

I slip into the heavy undergrowth and am away from everything but the river and its dense banks; I move slowly and fish, either with spinner or fly, every nook and pool I can reach by any means. I especially linger near those most difficult to fish. I shall not tell you how many holdover trout I take, or average, or see— only that for me it is worthwhile. And it is as solitary as any unnamed creek in the Northwest Territories.

Some of the river's minor secrets are themselves impressive. The lower river, so high and impossible to fish during the first weeks of the season, becomes—unlike the upper river—a flyfisherman's delight in the late spring, summer, and fall. Looking at the river in early April, you would not believe this, but should you drive by it a month later (three miles of the best water skirts the highway in plain sight), you would be quickly convinced.

The submerged boulders could not be seen in early spring; there was only the high, white-ruffled, muddy flow, unbroken on the surface. But now the rocks stand high and there are a thousand little covers and runs in a mile of auburn water, each with its trout or two. These will be hatchery trout, most of them; but a full 30 percent will be holdovers. They rise readily to the fly when the water is cool enough. The water is never crystalline here, but there is no section of the now-shallow and pocketed stream where a dry fly cannot be fished comfortably.

The water is ten, twelve, perhaps fourteen feet lower than in the early spring; an exceptional number of fish will have survived the early onslaught; and because the stream has shrunk so substantially, each fishable pocket probably contains several trout.

Still, they are not so easy to take as one might suppose.

For several weeks after the water has dropped and while the water is still cold, you can fish a wet fly or streamer fruitfully in the pockets and riffles. The gradient is sharp and the water fast; it is quick, concentrated fishing during those few weeks when the water is low and still cold, but often highly productive. A bad rain and of course the fishing is ruined for several weeks; several years the water went from high and muddy to low and warm, and there was none of this fine wet-fly fishing.

Since Big Muddy is not fed by springs, and since it flows through miles of open cow pastures, the water heats up quickly and remains warm throughout much of the season. In mid-May and June, most fly-fishermen try it in midmorning or in the evening.

Wrong.

When the water warms, the fish go deep under the rocks; they grow sluggish during the day and even during the rare substantial hatches they will not always move. Dusk this far from the mountains cannot quite cool the river enough, so evening fishing is not what it can be in June on the Beaverkill or Battenkill. The fish become a bit more active, but rarely hysterical in their feeding. Perhaps the night is the best time; I do not know, for it is difficult to fish any water at night and this river, with its many boulders and small pockets, requiring deft wading and pinpoint casts, has never lured me after dark.

But early morning?

Very early morning?

Yes, during the summer, if you are willing to be on the stream at four or four thirty, then perhaps you will have a few hours of the lower river at its best during the dog days. The water is cool and clear; mists swirl off the surface slowly, with not an angler in sight. Even the highway is silent. But the fish are all moving: you can see them darting everywhere in the shallow stream.

I have fished the stretch bordering the highway, which is by far the most pleasant that Big Muddy affords, for three hours in the early mornings of summer and taken ten to fifteen decent trout. During the first weeks of the season, perhaps five hundred fishermen at a time line these same banks and, catching almost nothing, blame poor stocking; an hour after I leave, at seven, the traditional fly-fishermen will arrive—and score only modestly.

I have taken a good number of surprising holdover browns in this stretch—up to sixteen inches. The fishing is a brand I much like: dry-fly fishing in low, fast pocket water where casts must be short and deft, where the fly comes down quick and bouncy, where strikes are sudden and electric, and a trout on means a spirited fight in fast water with complex currents and limited space in which to play your fish. Since this is my own Early Morning (and Usually Weekday) Private Club, I usually return the fish I catch in this lower section.

I also fish the upper river in the early mornings of summer. I travel light, with sneakers and khakis, a light Zealon jacket, no net, one box of flies, a cotton hat pulled down all around. I have not moved one of the truly large ones yet, the old cannibals, but I may: I dream of doing so. But I usually take one or two good fish from the riffles around five o'clock, and perhaps see or touch several others. It is enough.

Most convenient and most pleasant of all fishing on Big Muddy is autumn angling in the lower river—late autumn angling. The water is then uniformly cool throughout the day, the fish are all an inch or more large, they are moving and looking and shoring up for the winter—and, most pleasant, most fishermen have completely given up the stream by this time.

The birches are ablaze, the willows are yellow, and their long slender leaves glide down the riffles like so many gnomes' boats, the air is cool, and the action is fast. On a Saturday in late September, I can usually fish those same few miles of water bordering the highway, in midday, at my own convenience, and see perhaps one or two other fishermen. It is a time to share Big Muddy with a close friend, to finish out the season with a bit of talk, a lunch on the banks, a few fat trout in the creel. Except for the highway, we might be in Maine or Nova Scotia: it is that quiet and peaceful and productive on Big Muddy, on a genial Saturday when we have risen late, taken three hours to drink our last of the season, and shared a few dreams.

There are sections of Big Muddy I have never fished, for it is a long and winding river: that for two miles below the town; the upper cow pasture section above the upper region; its last mile, before it is lost in a large sea-funneling stream. On the maps it is more than twelve miles long—enough for a lifetime.

Someday I hope to catch the upper river in late autumn, when there has been no rain for a month, when the rips are pleasant riffles and the water crisply cold, when there has been a particular kind of drizzle and the water has turned slightly. Then, perhaps, I shall fish a Grey Fox Variant into the head of a deep pool, standing on the branches of a once-submerged tree, and draw one of the cannibals to the fly.

It is worth the dreaming.

For the scorn heaped upon it, Big Muddy has been generous to me; and if I cannot love it, I still value its special challenge, its special secrets. It keeps my childhood fresh and it still provides excitement within hours of home. It may not be a worthy mistress for my wife to envy, but it is close enough that I can make her a fishing widow for less time. Fished in its back reaches, at odd hours, at odd seasons, it can be exceptional.

Each river has its own music, its own song. The lowliest and nearest of them, the Big Muddys, have their music too.

13

My Secret Life

 I HAD NOT WANTED TO REMAIN IN THE
stream late. I had wanted to meet the ecstat-
ic rise I was confident would appear again
in the July dusk, and then be back at the inn
shortly after nine, making the best of two worlds. We were away
for a long weekend without the children. An infrequent business.
It was not to be a second honeymoon—but we had our plans.

We had spent a long day shopping and playing tourist in
Manchester, and in the late afternoon my wife had insisted we
could not pass through our brief vacation without at least one leisurely meal together at the inn: meals came with the price of the
room and were reputed excellent. We had missed them all. Why
did fishing always take place at odd hours? Afterward, she suggested, there might be other treats that middle-aged folk are still
heir to.

We were seated at six, and it may be that the waitress, who arrived late and flushed, had other affairs in the kitchen. I thought she'd never come. When she did, my wife said: "Let's have a drink first. I want to relax." My wife takes apricot liqueur. She takes it slowly.

The meal was a model of leisurely eating: a fifteen-minute wait for the fruit cup; a seven-minute wait for the empty cup to be taken away; salad served separately; twenty-three minutes for my wife's chicken to be cooked to order; a thoughtful few minutes selecting from the spice and cheese plate; warm comments on the charm of the spice and cheese plate; a long small dessert. And then, about ten to eight, my wife had done more than linger leisurely over her cup of coffee: she had lingered leisurely over three cups of coffee, the clock on the wall spinning madly, my heart heavy, my whole chest choked up with a lump the size of an avocado.

For I had fallen feathers and bamboo for the Battenkill and her sweeping glides and rose-moled trout. I had fished her enough during our three days in Vermont to know that I could not resist her. She had coaxed my deepest passions, won my heart. She had played the coquette with me, teased me with her ample hatches and selective trout. But I had felt, all day, in this curio shop and that basket barn, that I now knew enough of her mysteries to do some business with her that evening. The day had been warm and overcast; if it did not rain the evening would be sensuous and full.

"Well," I said, rising vigorously and patting my stomach. "I'm delighted you suggested this. An absolutely delicious meal. Delicious."

"I'm not done with my coffee, Nick."

"Third cup," I said. "Bad for your liver."

"A few more minutes. Please, Nick? It's been so pleasant. I really didn't believe you'd actually do it—have dinner with me."

I sat down on the corner of my chair, smiled, and drummed my fingers a few times. I *had* promised a leisurely meal.

"Do you have to?"

"What?"

"Drum your fingers and tap your foot? It makes me nervous.''

"It's ten after eight.''

"And you want to catch the match, or whatever you do.''

"Yes. Yes, actually I do. It's been a wonderful day. Wonderful. Great meal. Great.'' I smiled with infinite sweetness, rose, told her to sign the check, told her to have another coffee, two more coffees, told her I'd meet her in an hour and a half, that I loved her, that I'd always love her, more than anything—and then I bolted.

No doubt I drove recklessly down the grey highway with its drab gas stations and gaudy motels, but I hit no one and only ran the wheels off onto the gravel siding twice. I was suited up and heading on down the steep bank at precisely eight twenty-three.

Through the spruce and birch and alders, down past the rocky ledges, I could see her and hear her: the river. Clouds of flies were coming off the surface, rising against the dun blue of the evening sky. The sun had already dropped below the rim of the western mountains and a breathless calm hung over the valley of the Battenkill.

I scurried down the slope to what I had named Marietta's Pool, after the name of the man who owned a house on its high bank. I have since infancy watched rivers from the corner of my eye, from speeding cars, and I had first spotted this run in this way. I had named it for myself, as I had named a hundred others —their names secret and hallowed and storied.

It was a breathtaking run of several hundred yards: a series of quick twists and angular turns along a sharp gradient, an undulating series of deepening riffles opening into a magnificent pool farther across than could be cast, deeper than could ever be known fully. There were overhanging willow branches on the opposite side, and, as the stream widened, almost no possibility of wading —since the water flowed deep and flush to the banks. On the side I fished, the only side that was fishable, the water coursed against the bank with true velocity: the drop-off was sheer and probably lethal. For a hundred broad yards, there were numerous portions that simply could not be reached, areas that had to offer fine and permanent cover. I had seen a mounted nine-pound trout that came from the Battenkill on a spinner; it might well have come from such a pool.

Its tail was long and flat and wide—the water no more than three feet deep at any spot. In the mornings, when the mist swirled from the surface, I had seen large fish cruising in these flats; but I had not been wise enough to raise one. Working upstream I had been surprised, at midmorning, to see, in the very deepest water, the steadily pocked water of generously feeding fish. And I had seen the ecstatic evening rise the night before, fished over it for two hours without pricking a fish. It was a pool of many and subtle moods.

I waded in along the boulder bank where the water was deep and slow and full, feeling the cold thrust of the heavy current against my waders. I took a bit of water along my left leg, felt its sharp chill, and noted that it came in below the knee.

Then I began to inch downstream, where the fish were working steadily in mid-current. It was treacherous work. I had to manipulate my feet along the tops of high and mossy rocks, in fast current, at dusk, where a wrong step could mean far more than a bad spill; to the sides of the boulders I stepped on, the water might easily be ten feet deep. But the fish were working twenty yards downstream and there was no other way to approach them. The river's most evocative parts were the hardest to penetrate. I wanted to be even with them, perhaps downstream of the great feast.

The dusk was now sensuous and ripe. The stream birds glided in quick parabolas through the clouds of dancing mayflies, pausing and fluttering when their bills found a soft ephemera. The fish, all native browns, were not rising so much as lolling several inches below the surface, waiting for the nymphs to rise to them or for the duns to fall back and ride the little waves. The surface of that deep center water, with its sinewy currents, boiled without pause. I could see the tails and fins of the fish shift a foot, two feet, to take a hatching or floating dun. From every safe covert and cover, every fish in the run must have been lured mindlessly to the top for this sweet and leisurely feed.

I had been told there was no Cahill hatch on the Battenkill, but, catching one of the whirling duns in my hand, the species seemed close enough for me: perhaps a bit creamier, but I would have to prefer the mandarin wings to the unmarked hackle of a Cream Variant here. I had tied a dozen Cahills with cream hackle and cream bodies; they work well on the Amawalk. My clumsy flies seemed a reasonable imitation of this too easily crushed little insect in my hand, a fair bait.

There is a rhythm to the Battenkill, a haunting music in its ways. As I worked downstream, grasping this alder branch and that for support, probing tentatively with my feet before I made any step, I could feel it: an undulating pattern of sound and sight. Perhaps it is the clear meted flow, the deep glides, the incessant slurping of the trout; perhaps the birds and fish feel it, live in it, create it: but it is there. I could feel it and tried to enter it.

By the time I had reached a position slightly downstream of the main feeding area, the dusk was nearly set in; there was only a greyish glow in the sky. The feeding had reached an excited yet curiously unhurried pitch; the scene had the frenzy and stillness of Poussin's *Rape of the Sabines*.

I cast several times, without haste, and soon took and released a firm ten-inch trout. Beneath a low-slung willow a heavier fish was rising in a fixed area and I lengthened my casts to reach it. I could not quite do so, so I probed with my feet and found several boulders beneath the deep water that would keep me emerged only slightly above my waist. My felts held, and though I could not now readily reach back and grasp a branch should I slip, I felt safe enough to manage a few long casts from this perch. I was intent now upon doing so. The large fish, or several fish, made huge slurping patterns beneath the willow.

The extra feet toward them and the added room for a back cast were enough. I made one short cast, let it ride out the float, and then shot the line within a foot of the rise area. The trout took instantly and leapt three times in rapid succession: high, twisting, breaking the rhythm of the stream electrically. By the time I brought him to net, after he had drawn line from the reel four times in heavy runs, darkness had settled into the borders and alley of the stream—and also a chill breeze.

I killed the brown, creeled it, and then tucked the rod under my arm. I had taken a slight shiver, from the water in my boots, the absence of enough warm clothing near my chest, the slightly spent feeling after an intense closing with a good fish. My mouth was sticky and dry; I cupped my hands and drew several small quick drinks from the river: they were sweet and cold.

The moon was not full. I could not see it, but remembered the honeydew arc I had seen the night before. Through the lattice-work of the branches, now radically changed to weighty shadows and abstractions, masses and patches of some deftly crafted tapestry, streams of light lit the surface of the river enough for me to see that flies were still coming off and that fish were still taking them. The adult mayflies were playing out the last hours of their brief lives—rising up out of the cool depths in swarms, dancing in crazy flight over the stream, fluttering into nearby branches. Now and again the gauzelike wings would catch a fraction of the light; in the dark they were mating and dancing their life's sole song, dipping to deposit eggs, fluttering and falling back to the water whence they had only recently emerged, fulfilled and spent.

At the inn, my wife was expecting me. But I could not yet leave. Too far out into the cool and heavy water, I packed a pipe, lit it, and stood for a moment listening to the river and the fish and the birds. I stood alone in the cave that was the stream's alley, a long winding covert cut from black woods, its form elusive and not entirely safe from the encroaching darkness. My pipe's pocket was a bright orange glow; several bits of tobacco sputtered out, stung my hand lightly and disappeared in the river.

When I cast again, I could not see the fly but only the streak of the white line on the surface. Several times I saw the line twitch, and struck—coming up fast with a bent and throbbing rod. I do not remember how many trout I brought to net, perhaps five or six, but I killed one more and remember that the action was intense and exhilarating. I stopped when I lost my second fly and leader tippet on a back cast. I could not, even holding a big Wulff fly against the sky, fit the heavy leader point in the eye; and, my hands shaking now, I could not tie on a new tippet.

Working my way back, with every deceptive shadow a possibly final trap, I realized with stark clarity quite how dangerous a position I had put myself in. The thirty yards back upstream to where I had entered took a half hour or more. I slipped twice, caught a branch, scratched my face and tugged a rip in my waders, and finally reached the familiar birch clump exhausted and severely shaking. I lit another pipe at the car and sat stone still for ten minutes—weary and spent.

My wife was reading in bed and did not look up when I entered. *Done it again,* I thought. *Insulted her, neglected her, let the fever lure me away.* She looked lovely: thoughtful, beautiful, warm.

I put my gear carefully in the bathroom—vest and hat and creel. I flexed the kinks in my shoulders and felt the deep tiredness throughout my body. I flushed my face with cold water, combed out my matted hair, and changed my shirt for a pajama top. In the corner, against the wall, I leaned my uncased and disjointed rod.

"Mari?"

She did not answer but lay, face from me, deep in her book. I plucked a fly out of the lamb's wool patch on my vest, clipped the excess leader, and placed it with others of its kind. "Mari?"

"In a minute. In a minute."

I finished a few more chores and then opened the creel for another look at the two browns I had kept. Their spots were still bright red. The cool evening air had kept them fresh. They were considerably larger than I had first thought.

"Whew," my wife said loudly. "Tolstoy is incredible. You wouldn't believe the way he can make a scene come alive." She twisted on the bed, smiled, and then jumped off and toward me. "Catch anything?"

I held the open creel toward her.

"They're exquisite. I've never seen such bright coloration. It must have been an exciting evening for you. What time is it?"

Later, when the lights were out and we were close in the bed, she said: "Of course I don't mind if you fish. Wouldn't do any good if I did. I've learned that much. And I'm happy when you

are. It was a delicious dinner, and reading Tolstoy in a warm bed
is a lot better than being bitten to shreds by bugs along one of your
streams.''

We lay touching in the dark room, listening to a car pass now
and then, a muffled voice in another room, applause and laughter
from a television set in another world.

"Nick." I heard the word but did not answer. "Nick?"

"Yes."

"I'm going to get a secret lover, too," she whispered flatly.
"The Empire State Building or something. You'll see. I'll meet it
at night, and dream about it." She sighed and pulled me closer. I
could smell her fresh perfume; I felt her hair against my cheek.
"Meanwhile, I guess you'll do. Even if you are a madman. And
an adulterer.''

I felt my mouth widen in a smile. I changed position and put
my lips to the soft nape of her neck. Eyes closed, I could not help
but see the river at dusk, and after dusk, and I could still feel her
undulating rhythms on my mind and thighs. I wondered if the
hours between twelve and six were as generous.

NIGHT FISHING

The shadows blur, the waxwings
swoop and dip; the eye is all,
the dunnish sky is hushed and quick.
Beyond the water's warbling song
you hear the slurp and chop
of feeding fish—prelude
to a symphony of quiet
when this swift river goes all still
and slow in flowing timelessness.

And then you ply the darker dark
beneath the dark, in soft pursuit
and deft and gentle renderings,

seeking a thing outside, within
the ripe unconscious of the stream
or you—
   until you are not there
but pantheized into a thousand
warbling sounds without shadow.

14

Present
for an Angler

MY SON,

This is the season for gift giving, the time at which friends present to friends some message of their affection. It is the cold season, when we hibernate and survive on dreams, as bears lick their paws in winter.

I have thought for months of what would best suit this moment. You are too old for toys, all my books are already yours, and we now share fly-fishing tackle, of which there has been—since before you were born—a superabundance.

Money will not suit.

Nor, I think, will anything material this year.

For we have mingled our dreams these past months, our words have sometimes been one, we have smiled deeply into each other's eyes.

There were other moments, too: days when we edged around each other, like boxers in a ring, yet fearing to intrude on the other's somewhat mysterious domain. We are neither the same age nor of the same time. I remember those moments when blood boiled, when we did not smile at each other. For you are nearly a man now—and will go your own way, which is not always my way, as men must.

I remember, too, how we sat on a ruffled lake, probing the pea green depths for fish that never came, and how uneasy we both grew: you wanting action, I wanting the action for you that I had promised. I remember the float trip we took down the Madison River, and how, in a channel, beside a guide not much older than yourself, you took your first trout on a fly. By yourself. Without help. It was a fine, brightly spotted brown, and if you fought him a little too long, that only increased my pleasure in watching. Your eyes sparkled then, grew serious as you edged him gingerly toward your net, as if he was a treasure—which he was. I remember how we lifted the net high, smiled deeply, and how we carefully returned the fish and watched it weave away.

I think you would have liked to keep that trout. When I was fifteen, I'd have killed him on the spot. But you returned him, without my urging, and I was proud: for the rivers need men who will return their treasures.

I remember that afternoon we drove into the valley of the Little Snake, and how much farther the trip was than we'd thought—over a ragged, rocky road, twisting and hilly, for two hours without sight of water large enough to hold a decent bullfrog. I may not have agreed openly with your desire to turn back, but turning back was on my mind for more than an hour. And yet we kept going, edged on by a rumor, a dream, some faint expectations—as men must pursue their dreams, of all kinds, even when dreams seem wrecked.

I doubt if you will ever forget what we found. The river was cool and quick that hot summer day, and the valley was isolated: we had pressed beyond the hordes who seek easy, stocked rivers, to some isolated place where the trout grew wild. We could feel it.

I doubt if you will ever forget what is now *our* pool—the one upstream from the farm.

We'd brought only one fly rod, and you began to fish the tail of the pool first. I liked the progress you'd made with your fly-fishing—the way your wrist stayed firm and the line curled high behind you, the way you brought in line as the fly floated down toward us, the two of us standing side by side, me at your left elbow.

And then we saw a good fish flash in the current, at the head of the pool, breaking the water with a quick white spurt, as these western fish often will. We headed upstream quickly, until you could reach that spot with a comfortable cast, and then we both watched as the Rio Grande King bobbed down in the current until, suddenly, with a little flash that sent big shivers into us, it disappeared.

You struck late.

And then you struck late again and turned to me, quizzically.

On the third strike you raised the rod high when the fish took, felt the line stay taut, and turned to me in disbelief and radiance. Remember?

How can I forget?

Not the stern look of determination nor the flooding smile. Never the wild elation that swept through us when that fish leaped once, twice, three times in rapid succession, bore deep, and finally came to your net. Nor the broad, unfettered smiles that sprang from us both, as alternately, we took five, six—was it finally seven?—of those bright river-bred, leaping rainbows.

We went back once more, several days later, each with his own fly rod. The river was lower and we didn't expect to repeat that first day. You went off by yourself, the first time you had to manage the whole complicated ritual of fly-fishing alone. Several times, from downstream, I saw your rod arced. Twice I saw you bend over with the net, in the classic pose. I was doing some business of my own, and did not see it all, but in the end you had taken six by yourself that day, up to sixteen inches—and you'd also learned that the points break off hooks when they're snapped back against the rocks, that sunglasses and other small items have an ornery habit of falling out of one's vest, that reliable knots are hard to tie, that even fly lines can get hopelessly snarled. Not forever, Paul. Once you couldn't cast a fly line.

We drove back in the darkness that night, both knowing you'd never be a fishing widow again, and counted thirteen deer in the fields—lithe, loping creatures of the meadows and forests.

I remember, too, the day we climbed high above Fish Creek Falls. The river was small and fast, pocketed with swirling crystalline pools, and the narrow trail climbed far back into the woods and sharply up. You loped, I lumbered. You chattered, I panted. After an hour, we found a small pool and cast several times each. We caught two little brookies—maybe four inches long—but do you remember their colors? Bright red and black—their bellies golden orange. How flipping and frisky and cold they were, and how quick-darting when we returned them to the stream. Remember, Paul?

It is grey and dry as the moon here in the city. Winter's here, and even the snow will not be bright white. It is the gift-giving season, and I have given the matter some thought. But what can I present to you in return for such brightly colored memories?

What more than the hope that you share them, too, my son?

Part Three

FISHING WIDOWS

15

Fishing Widows

A TALE

"En amour c'est comme dans la pêche, c'est le plus patient qui gagne."

THE DECISION TO SPEND OUR VACATION on the Middle Branch could scarcely have pleased my wife less. She was never partial to fish or fishing camps or, as a class, to fishermen. But we had traded a week on the Cape for two weeks on the river. I had fulfilled my end of the bargain nobly, I thought—wasn't I pocked like a leper from the sun, still scratching the poison ivy, and penny poor?—and now she promised to be brave. I was as anxious to see *that* as I was the dusk hatch of *Potamanthus:* Jane had never made a brave or patient fishing widow.

I had made reservations at the Cloverleaf, a modest but comfortable little motel that catered primarily to fishermen and their families. The Middle Branch is not an easy river and I had fished it, with limited success, only twice before; I wanted to stay at a place where a few evening drinks might loosen profitable informa-

117

tion about this or that pool or run that was hot, or special flies. During the long trip up from the city, I tried assiduously not to think of *la pêche,* but Jane caught the telltale turn of my head each time we passed a river, and frowned. We arrived at five thirty, registered, and went directly to our room. It was small but immaculate, and there were fishing prints on the walls and ashtrays, and the lampshades were decorated with flies or rising trout. The rooms didn't have numbers: ours was called Blue Dun. I had stayed there once before, by myself, and the familiar quiet surroundings helped give me an immediate sense of that peace I seek from my fishing. Jane thought the art was lousy.

Dinner was served at a long cherrywood table and we found ourselves with a companion at either side. To my left sat a tall, distinguished man in his early sixties, with clear white hair, a neat touch of a white-grey moustache, and impeccable manners. He had that supreme self-control that marks a man successful in finances and life.

"Allen C. Lord," he said, introducing himself.

"Jack Brooks," I said.

He too had come up from the city that afternoon. We got on immediately, trading a few stories he had heard about the river for a few of my previous experiences. He spoke knowledgeably but a bit compulsively about flies and rods and lines, and I fell into that easy and infectious ambiance of enjoying someone who shares a common passion—particularly when it is the mystique of trout fishing.

There were two women at the other end of the table, both in their late fifties and obviously long-time friends; they had come up with their husbands—both of whom, we learned, had passed up dinner for the fourth straight night to be on the river—and with them was a strikingly beautiful young woman. The young woman talked with impatient animation, and her eyes kept darting down the table and toward the door, as if she were distracted or bored or looking for someone.

To Jane's right sat a handsome woman of about fifty-five; she spoke to no one at first, but after a while—perhaps because I was speaking to Lord so avidly, and ignoring my wife—she and Jane began to talk. I simply heard their voices, not what they were saying, because Lord had begun a rather interesting and elaborate story about a man who fished with spinning lures, with the hooks cut off, in order to locate trout he later took with flies.

"The man was an incredibly good fly-fisherman, you see," said Lord, "but he liked nothing better than to fish new and difficult waters—big waters that no man could read easily. This was twenty-five years ago, when spinning first came in, and he carried a short telescopic rod and a tiny European reel. I saw him heading out to the river once with that outfit strapped to his belt and called him to account for it. I suppose what I'd meant as playful chiding came through as a rebuke, for he bristled and told me to mind my own goddam business—which I usually do. Well, I apologized, he apologized, and then he invited me to fish with him that afternoon. What a remarkable sight. I didn't have the slightest idea he was using lures without hooks, since I was some distance off. He worked his way quickly up a long fast run, casting a short low line constantly with pinpoint accuracy, and every now and then his rod would bow over sharply and then snap back. That must have happened eight or nine times. When he'd finished, he went up into the woods on the opposite side of the river, and emerged at the tail of the run. There he sat down on a rock, smoked a pipe, and studied the water, stark still as a blue heron. Fifteen minutes later, he set up a fly rod he'd placed there earlier. It took him two hours to work up that same stretch of water, flicking his fly deftly and selectively. At first I didn't realize there was a pattern to it, but it soon became apparent that he was fishing the areas in which he had previously located a good fish. Not the exact spot, either—but to the spot he knew the fish must have been holding to have taken the lure where they did. He took eight trout, all good size, and returned each; later, he made me swear not to reveal the kind of spinning lure he used. Too deadly. I haven't, of course, to this day. What amazed me most was his instant recall of where the trout were in that long run and . . ."

"But was that fair?" It was a woman's voice, and came from the other side of my wife.

"Hello?" said Lord.

"I'm sorry," said the woman, "but do you think all that was quite ethical?"

"Don't see why not, no," said Lord. "Quite ingenious. Anyway, the man had a perfectly dreadful wife who didn't fish, and he never got on the water nearly enough. He didn't have time to spend weeks searching for fish. He had to find them quickly, if he wanted any fish at all."

Jane frowned and grunted; I changed the subject. "Something like using a loss leader for bait in business."

"Not at all," said Lord. "But what was the man to do? His wife had cut him down to a miserly eight or ten fishing trips a year. He was under the gun."

"Ingenious, yes." The woman was leaning beyond Jane now, and peering down the table intently at Lord. "But would *you* do it?"

Lord smiled. "In business, yes. For trout, no."

"I respect you for that, sir," she said. She sounded the perfect purist. I was impressed.

"But I never learned to use a spinning rod," said Lord. "And my memory is poor. Quite poor."

"Mrs. Warren is an excellent fisherwoman," said Jane. My wife had adamantly refused to try the sport once.

"Not *quite* excellent, my dear—but certainly enthusiastic."

"Very interesting," said Lord. "Does your husband fish?"

"Mr. Warren was an enthusiast—and an expert—right to the end."

"Gone?" asked Lord. "I'm sorry."

"Don't be. He died . . . with his boots on, as they say."

"Not along a stream?"

The two of them were leaning far around Jane and me, and we pushed our chairs back so they could talk more conveniently. I couldn't reach my plate of roast beef, and, knowing Jane disliked fish talk, took her hand and smiled. But she was intensely interested in the discussion for some reason. I noticed then that all the plates were monographed with rising trout; I had a splendid rainbow on mine, Jane a brown.

"Yes," said Mrs. Warren. "Along a stream. Heart attack.

Very sudden. And they found two good trout in his creel.''

"Remarkable," said Lord.

"He would have chosen to go that way. I wasn't with him that time, though we often fished together.''

I had visions of the two Warrens fishing on the lovely Middle Branch—man and wife—exchanging lore, taking samples of fly life together, tying flies together in the winter. I had grown to view my fishing life as so separate from anything I would ever share with my wife that the thought of these two intrigued me. There was a touch of the idyll to it: Theodore Gordon and the mysterious girl in that photograph taken on the Neversink. A rare poetry. It transcended the conscious and unconscious male chauvinism I'd seen so much of—and fallen into myself—and wifely bitchiness.

Coffee hadn't come but it was, I saw on the wall clock, seven already. "Well," I said, rising quickly, "I'll just head off now. I want to be on the water by seven thirty, Jane. You don't mind?"

"Fishing the lower water?" asked Lord.

"No. Near the pasture, I think. I raised a really good brown there two years ago and . . .''

Lord laughed heartily.

"No," I said, "I guess he won't be there—but I've dreamed of that run. And some spots *do* remain productive, you know.''

"That's quite so," said Mrs. Warren.

"Some wives like their coffee," said Jane. "After every meal." She said it lightly; there were strangers present.

"Is there enough water for two?" Lord asked.

"Absolutely. Shall we go together?"

We agreed to do so, and Jane decided to come along with us rather than remain at the unfamiliar motel alone. We rose from the table together, Jane frowning privately at me, when she thought the others couldn't see. Mrs. Warren rose also and said good-bye and good luck to us all. It never occurred to me to ask her to join us, though in retrospect I recall detecting a certain sense of awkwardness, as if, perhaps, though I could not be sure, she expected Lord or me to invite her. Surely that would have been the case had we all been men.

As we drove off ten minutes later, I noticed Mrs. Warren walking to her car. She held a vest in one hand and a metal rod tube in the other. There was a wistful sadness in the sight, and I thought again of that lost poetry, of her and Mr. Warren and how many times they must have headed off silently together to fish the dusk rise. I didn't notice whether Lord was watching her, but I doubt it: he was walking and talking too quickly to have poetry on his mind.

We had a fine evening. Jane took a book and went off on a rock to read. No defined hatch ever materialized, but a few fish were working here and there, and I enjoyed casting to them. I had no more than three slap rises, I pricked one fish, lost another, and then, just at dusk connected with a fine native brown of fourteen inches that jumped three times and several times stripped line from the reel before I netted him.

Lord was working ahead of me, pipe in mouth, and I had the distinct sensation that I was watching a man totally at peace with the world. His posture, his gestures revealed his intensity and pleasure. That he raised not a fish didn't seem to trouble him a bit. The brighter sky above the treeline was cut now and then by a swallow dipping and maneuvering in flight to catch some insect; the air became sharp and chill; the crickets, with their long shrill song, surrounded us. Three or four times I watched Lord, with his back toward me, tuck his long rod under his arm, take a box out of one of the pockets in his vest, and tie on a new fly. He seemed to enjoy the process. Then he was casting again, and the long line lofted back, curled, and rode forward with decision.

"Splendid evening," Lord said in the car, flexing his tired shoulders back as I slowly turned the car and headed out of the woods along the dirt road. "Didn't move a thing, but it didn't matter. I work like a son of a gun all week. Business lunches and board meetings and crises—you wouldn't believe the crises!—and there's nothing I enjoy more than being off like this on a good river. You know, I really don't care, on a night like this, if I catch anything or not. That's a beautiful stretch of water, isn't it?"

"I'd love to hit it when a really good hatch is on."

"Say, where's your wife, old man?"

I struck the brake sharply, stopped and slapped my forehead. "No-no-no," I muttered. I threw the car into reverse and backed zigzaggedly down the road in a sweat.

She was sitting on a rock by the side of the road, in the dark. The headlights caught her and she shielded her face. It was swollen from crying and from the mosquitoes, and she was biting her lower lip.

Two

"Of course she should have known better," said Lord at breakfast, introducing the subject immediately, "than to sit outside without protection of any kind."

"She can't stand the smell of those repellents," I said glumly.

"But there's a lot you could do, too," he advised. "I once knew a man with a similar problem . . ."

"Were you ever married?" I asked.

"Never. Confirmed bachelor. Well, I told him I'd give his problem a lot of thought, and I did. I realized that the bugs were the biggest problem, so I found a repellent that smelled like Chanel Number Five. And I knew that a car could be damned uncomfortable, so I suggested he buy an aluminum chair. I told him to make sure she always had a thermos of coffee—your lady like coffee?—and plenty of good books."

I nodded.

"And a radio."

"Jane doesn't like the radio."

"Well, something of the kind. Get her something to keep her mind busy, to kill time for her. That's what I suggested."

He sounded like a professional coach, and I wondered how many other young married men he'd advised—from his insulated bachelorhood. And whether his system would work with Jane.

"I insisted he get her a hood of mosquito netting. He'd always been one to rush off quickly and hit the stream as soon as possible, but I taught him to get there earlier than usual and then to spend a half hour making sure his little lady was comfortable and had everything she wanted. I even coached him to say, in a leisurely manner, that he thought he'd head down the river a bit, if his wife didn't mind; of course once he hit the woodline he'd fall into a trot, but how could she know that?''

"Did it work?''

"Like a charm. Most of the time. You can't plan on it raining, of course. And once he sat her right on top of a red anthill.''

"The point,'' I said quietly, "is that Jane can't stand to kill time, she prefers to read on a couch or soft chair, and hates bugs, whether they finally bite her or not. She does like her coffee, though, and I suppose I could . . .''

"Well, you adjust the specifics, old man. There's nothing fixed and firm about my plan. The point is, find some way to keep them out of your hair. It just takes a little intelligent planning.''

"The point is,'' I said, "that Jane hates everything connected with fishing and cannot see one iota of the fascination to a grown man of catching dumb fish. Why all the talk, all the tinkering with tackle, all the books, all the fly tying, all that anxiety as to whether or not the Hendricksons or Cahills will be on or off this or that afternoon, she asks me.''

"Difficult questions,'' said Lord meditatively.

"Impossible questions,'' I said. I looked around to see if Jane had come in, and then continued, my voice growing a little shrill. "I try to explain to her about rivers—how each is different; she says books and people and works of art are different, too. I tell her about the composition of the riverbed, whether of rock, pebbles, sand, or mud; the color of the water; the placement of particular rocks, and what they do to the current; the presence of a tree, impeding, redirecting the flow; the special ecology of each river—the kinds of mayfies it holds, when they hatch, the *lawfulness* of their hatching cycles; the animals that frequent the river's banks. You know, the thousand variables . . .''

"And what does she say?''

" 'Read any good books lately? Gone to a museum?' "

"I see how it is, old man," he said, putting his hand on top of mine, "but an intelligent . . ." Then his head turned sharply. Mrs. Warren had come in. She looked absolutely splendid in her bright checkered shirt, tight slacks, and a striped Indian band around her forehead. She smiled at us and sat down several seats away.

". . . the thousand variables," I continued, "that make trout fishing such a marvelous mystery. Why can't she understand it?" My voice was rising again. "The fascination of it all?"

"Yes," Lord said, distractedly. He hadn't taken his eyes off Mrs. Warren. I could hear his brain humming. Suddenly he stood up and, without excusing himself, took two steps toward her and said: "Good morning, ma'am."

Jane was still sleeping; she had cried half the night and I'd decided not to wake her when I tiptoed out. Two men, the husbands of women I'd seen the night before, were finishing their coffee at the other end of the table. Through the window I saw a young man and the young woman I'd seen at dinner; they were talking intently to each other at a picnic table. He was dressed for the stream and had an aluminum rod case under his arm. She had on a lovely print dress; her hair was bobbed, and she was boiling mad.

Lord offered a few pleasantries to Mrs. Warren, but did not ask how she had done the evening before—though of course it was a logical question if someone, even a woman, had been out fishing. Then he turned back to me and began to talk of the water we intended to fish that morning, below the cemetery. He had read of it in an article some years ago, and since I'd had my choice the night before, we'd agreed to fish at his convenience this morning. He took his wallet out and produced a small, worn photograph of a strange fly. "It was mentioned in the article, and I had a dozen like it tied up last winter. Lend you several if you'd like."

I said I'd be pleased to try them, though they didn't look very representational to me. They had half-spent elk-hair wings, a grizzly palmered body, and a red tag.

"May I see that?" asked Mrs. Warren.

"Of course," I said, and leaned far down the table to hand it to her.

"Yes," she said. "The Blitz. Herbert used these and took a great many trout with them on the Middle Branch. It's a local pattern, and terribly effective in this area but nowhere else."

"Is that so?" asked Lord. "Fish the river often, did he?"

"We always vacationed here. Herbert loved the river."

"Take a lot of fish, did he?"

"He was an excellent fisherman."

Our bacon and eggs were brought in, on those trout-decorated plates, and placed before us. I began to eat mine at once. Lord did not.

"You wouldn't by any chance know any of his favorite spots, ma'am?"

"I fished with him. I know them all," she said without hesitation.

"All of them?"

"I believe so."

"Is that so?"

"You see, he kept detailed maps of the entire river, and"— she paused and took a sip of her orange juice—"even some rather comprehensive logbooks, with details on where he took fish, and what size they were, and what fly he took them on, and what time of . . ."

"Logbooks!" said Lord.

"Mr. Warren and I would spend the long winter evenings retyping and analyzing the maps and logbooks and thinking back over the many pleasant hours we'd spent on the river."

"Did I properly introduce myself last night? Name's Lord. A. C. Lord."

"Betty Warren."

Lord poked at a slice of bacon, broke it, couldn't get it onto his fork, and then picked it up with his fingers. "You wouldn't care to fish with us this morning, would you, Mrs.—Betty?"

"I wouldn't want to disturb you gentlemen."

"We'd be pleased, honored to have you along, wouldn't we?"

he said, nodding at me.

For myself, I would have preferred to fish alone. I don't like people watching me when I fish, and I like to move at my own pace. When I fish with experts, I invariably put a fly in my ear; when I fish with a novice, I'm forever unsnarling his leader. I'd come for a real rest, which I needed, and though Lord was pleasant to be with, I was rather thinking of ways to head off by myself in the afternoon. Three can be quite a crowd on most water, and I'd never fished with a woman. But Lord's equipment was still in my car, and I was rather curious to see this woman in action. She *had* to be a master.

We headed off about eight, the three of us sitting in the front, like old pals; I was at the wheel and Betty in the middle. Jane hadn't appeared by the time we left, and I was wondering whether or not I should have left a note. But what could I have said? It was a disaster, either way.

We hadn't gone a mile when Lord asked: "Betty, now I'm curious as to what *you'd* recommend on a morning like this."

"I'd head upstream, A.C.," she said quietly. "The other way. There's more shade and cover on the upper river, and the weather's a bit too warm for the Cemetery Run, I should think. Especially this time of the day. It gets the sun about this time, eight thirty, and if you're not there for a full hour or so before the sun hits it squarely, it's too bright and you don't get too much action."

"What do you think?" Lord asked me.

"Makes sense."

"Better turn around, don't you think?"

"It's your morning," I said, braking the car sharply.

Twenty minutes later, as we went slowly along the road bordering the upper river, waiting for some indication from our guide, Betty suddenly pointed to the right. "There. That's the spot. That break in the bush."

"No road there," I said, slowing down.

"It's not exactly a road, but it hasn't got many ruts and if you drive carefully it takes you right in near the Ledge Pool."

"Ledge Pool?" asked Lord.

"Never heard of it," I said.

"Sounds terrific."

"It's a lovely piece of water," said Betty.

"Heavily fished?" asked Lord.

"Hardly at all."

"Let's try it," said Lord.

The car broke through the close bushes and I headed it along an old dirt path, obviously not much used.

"Guess not too many fishermen get down this way," said Lord, half to himself.

"No, not many."

"The Ledge Pool's pretty good, you think, this time of the season, this time of day?"

"Your best bet, I should think," she said. "Don't use the Blitz here, though. A Cream Variant is best, quite large, up against the opposite bank. Skitter it if you can."

"I can skitter a variant," said Lord.

I edged the car along the path as far as I could, and then, on Betty's suggestion, turned toward the right and ended in a lovely little clump of birches, big enough for only one car. There were no tire tracks, and no cars could see us from the main road—and on a hard-fished stream like the Middle Branch!

We got out and Lord and I walked quickly to the top of a little rise. Below was one of the most magnificent pools I'd ever seen. The water came down fast out of a pinched bend and up against the long slate ledge, forming several eddies and quiet coves. The shallow head tapered quickly to a long pool of obvious depth, where the water slowed and the currents, flecked with bubbles, twisted languidly. It took my breath away. What was worse, we could see half-a-dozen solid rises up and down the pool.

"Good grief, man," said Lord in a hoarse whisper.

We looked at each other, "silent upon a peak in Darien." Then we bolted back to the car.

Betty was putting something back into her purse as we came up. I thought I saw the flash of a mirror but could not be sure. "Like it?" she asked.

"That is a magnificent piece of water," said Lord.

"Well, you two go along and I'll come down in a little bit," she said.

"Aren't you going to fish?" he asked.

"Perhaps a little later. I'd like to see you two get several first; I heard you didn't do too well last night."

"And you?" asked Lord. "I don't suppose you did much."

"I had a satisfactory evening," she said, snapping her purse shut.

"*Very* good?" asked Lord.

"Quite satisfactory, actually."

"You are a very interesting woman, Betty Warren," he said. "Extremely interesting."

"Why thank you very kindly," she said, genuinely pleased.

I let Lord get in ahead of me, at the tail of the pool, and told him I'd start up within fifteen minutes. I wanted to tie on a new tippet and piddle with some of my equipment. I'm usually first suited up and first into the water, but it was such a pleasant and mild day, and the water was so interesting, that I thought I'd do as the books say, for once, and study it first, before flailing away.

"Suit yourself," said Lord. He was quivering with electricity. He couldn't wait to get in.

I sat down on a rock, laid my rod up in the branches of some low willows, and dug out of the top pocket in my vest a spool of tippet material. Lord was casting almost before he'd stepped into the stream, false casting a short line rapidly back and forth—too rapidly. I could see he had his eye on a small boulder somewhat upstream. In a few moments he lengthened his back cast and shot the line out. I could not see the fly, which was lost in the shadows, but the end of his fly line reached to within seven or eight feet of the rock, a little to the left.

He held his rod tip high and retrieved with quick short jerks that made his fly skitter on the surface like a dancing insect. He brought it all the way in, whipped the fly off the surface, and began false casting again. I saw his head bend forward as he scrutinized the surface, and then his head nod as if he had seen the fish still rising.

Again he cast, this time well above the boulder, and again he skittered the fly along the surface.

I saw the boil of the fish before I saw Lord raise his arm to strike.

It was a big fish and had taken the skittered variant savagely. The rod was already high and there was somewhat too much shooting line coiled below the first guide: he had to rear back too far, and as he did so, he lost his footing and made a quick pedaling movement with his feet to regain his balance. He hung there for a moment—suspended, teetering—and then went down, caught himself with his left arm—all the time trying to hold his rod tip high—lost control again, and tumbled over onto his side in more than two feet of water.

I leaped and ran toward him.

He was thrashing around and trying to hold the rod high. But it was no good. The fish was off.

"By God, did you see that?" he asked, still down on his side in the water.

"Are you hurt?" I was genuinely concerned, for he wasn't a young man, and he'd taken a really bad fall.

"How big was it, do you think?"

I told him I had no idea, but that it looked to be a considerable fish. I asked again if he was all right.

"I never felt him," he said loudly. "I don't think I missed him—did I?—but the line was just too slack. I didn't really feel him."

I waded out to the man, who was still propped up on his left arm and helped him to his feet. "I saw him immediately," he said, "just below the boulder. As soon as I got near the water. And I knew he'd take if I got the fly to him properly." There was a thin line of blood trailing down his ear. He didn't notice it. "The first cast was short. I knew it was short. I doubt if he even moved for it. But I played it out. I could have ripped it off the surface, but I knew he'd go down if I did that. I had it figured just right: cast several feet *above*, mind you, *above*, the boulder; let the fly come down three or four feet dead drift; and *then* start skittering."

I noticed that the knuckles of his right hand were bruised, and also bloody.

"It worked perfectly," he said. "Did you see? Did you see him take it? What a rise! *That* was a real fish."

"Are you hurt?" I insisted.

"Who's hurt?"

"I asked if *you* were hurt."

"Never," he said, rubbing his left arm lightly. "Trouble is, Jack, I haven't taken a trout all year. Don't know what it is— overanxiousness, bad reflexes. Once I get the first one . . ." Then, suddenly, his eyes darted to the rim of the hill.

She was there, watching us both. Smiling slightly.

Lord breathed deeply and took notice, for the first time, of his condition. He was thoroughly soaked and his waders were filled to the thighs with the cold water. His hat had fallen off and he looked around for it; it was beached on the flats at the tail of the pool.

Betty Warren waved, but he turned his back and headed toward his hat. I waved back.

"Accident?" she called, her hands cupped to her mouth.

I nodded.

"Anybody hurt?"

"I don't think so," I called back.

"There are some fish rising up here near the head."

I turned and looked for Lord. He had retrieved his hat and was walking upstream through the willows, slowly, his head bent.

"We'll try for them later," I said.

I looked over to Lord, but he had disappeared back into the woods, so I walked back to the rock where I'd left my equipment and then arranged it and started after him.

Three

Though I had been kind beyond measure on the Cape, so kind Jane told me I was acting like an idiot—I could see that she was simply incapable of upholding her end of the bargain. The first night had been a horror; even if I followed Lord's ridiculous advice to the letter, there would probably be more disasters. Jane would not survive the two weeks intact without true magnanimity on my part.

So I did the magnanimous thing: I told her, when Lord and Betty Warren and I returned to the Cloverleaf, that she could have the entire day—until the dusk rise, of course—and that I'd be delighted to take her shopping.

"Don't the fishes bite in the afternoon?" she asked.

Lord had gone to his room, for a shower and rest; Betty Warren had politely seen us into the motel and then gone into town by herself. She was an exceptional woman. In the dining room, the two fishing couples were having lunch; the men were talking loudly about the morning's fishing and the women, sitting side by side, were speaking softly, in cowed tones. I didn't see the young man and woman.

The lunch table was handsomely set, with large bowls of apples, bananas, and grapes, a high vase full of bright red roses, and platters of neatly stacked sandwiches. The dishes at each setting were part of the trout set: flies on the salad plate, natural mayflies on the glasses, rising trout on the main plate.

"Want to eat here or out?" I asked Jane.

"Out. You invited me for a drive."

"We could go after lunch," I said.

She looked carefully at me for a moment and then into the dining room. I heard one of the men say "fourteen, fifteen inches, maybe . . ." and then caught snatches of animated talk about leader diameters and fly patterns, broken water and Green House pools. Jane kept watching me closely.

"Let's go in," I proposed, taking her arm. "Want to?"

"Not especially."

"Why not? We've paid for the meals," I whispered to her.

"I'd still like to go out, if you don't mind."

"But what's wrong . . ."

"It's the snake pit. That's what's wrong."

"All right. All right. If you want to go out, we'll go out. I only thought . . ."

"Then let's go," she said abruptly.

I put out my hand to touch hers, and half turned from the dining room. Lord had told me that these two men were positively experts—with reputations; I wanted to meet them, to ask how they'd done, to talk fishing with them.

"What are you men going to do this afternoon?" one of the women at the table asked.

"Go fishing," a deep voice answered.

"You fished all morning, Sam."

"I'm going fishing."

I felt my chest begin to tighten. Jane felt my hand try to touch hers and pulled it away. "Are you coming?" she asked in a low, dry voice.

"Go fishing," the deep voice in the dining room said again.

"All right, Jane," I said. "All right. We'll eat in town."

Four

It had been a wet summer for the Middle Branch valley. The foliage was thick and luxuriant along the banks of the river, and the river ran higher than I'd remembered it for this time of the year. The fly hatches had been delayed, and it took only half-a-dozen well-chosen questions to learn that the local fishermen were expecting some excellent fishing within the next few days, with multiple hatches and a receding river. You could see the best of them sitting along the banks, waiting—waiting like waxwings in the trees, like surf fishermen for the incoming tide.

Jane and I spoke little the next few days, though we were together constantly. We took breakfast alone, about nine thirty, after the others were already out, and then I'd fish alone or with Lord for an hour or two, no more, with singularly little success. I'd be back at the motel by twelve, to take her out to lunch: she did not want to eat in that dining room. In the afternoons, we drove sullenly through the exquisite countryside. I'd try to make conversation and she'd tell me not to try to make conversation. Several times, as we drove, I'd stop the car and look at a section of water. There were small dancing caddis everywhere, but the fish weren't coming to the top for them.

"Are you going fishing?" Jane would ask when I stopped the car.

"Nope."

"Isn't that why we came up here?"

"I suppose so."

"Then why don't you fish?"

"Maybe later."

"That's ridiculous. I know you're dying to fish. You know you're dying to fish. Why don't you get out your rod?"

"I just want to look at the water," I said. "Anyway, Lord says the fishing's been terrible. He hasn't caught a thing since he got up here."

And then I'd get out and look, and then go back to the car and start it up and drive about a bit more.

Thursday evening was warm and overcast., We'd gone to a corny summer-stock comedy in town the night before, and Jane said, about seven, that she'd just like to rest and read a book. "Fine," I said; "anything you say, Jane."

"What are you going to do?" she asked.

"Walk around a bit. Read a book. I don't know."

"Still being magnanimous?"

"What?" I said sharply.

She smiled. It was a genuinely warm smile. She took my hand. "Look, *please* go fishing. Fish all night if you want to. I don't want to go near one of those bug-infested rivers again as long as I live. But if that's what you want to do, do it. Go fishing. Go fishing"—she was smiling—"only don't walk around with that hangdog look for ten more minutes or I'll really never speak to you again. Not as long as I live."

"You mean it?"

"You don't need my permission to go fishing. Go. Get the hell out of here. Let me read my goddam book."

I leaned over and kissed her wetly on the cheek. Then I turned, walked a few steps, looked back at her, saw her smiling and shaking her head, waved, and trotted off.

I decided to try upstream, near several long flat pools I'd

discovered. My gear was all in the car, and I raced off, the pebbles churning as my tires skidded. No one was on the pool I wanted to fish, but I saw a familiar car from the motel; I thought it belonged to the two experts and their young friend.

I parked as far off the road and into the trees as I dared, where I could watch the water while I put on my waders and vest.

There was something magical about the river: the swallows were in the trees and I could hear their shrill peeps above the rush of the little falls at the head of the pool. The water was still; no fish were working. A bullfrog grunted from the rushes downstream; I saw a rabbit pause, then scamper off into the high grass.

I breathed deeply, sat propped against the right front fender of the car, and pulled up my waders. When they were on, and the suspenders adjusted, I picked my vest out from the carryall valise, checked my pockets for fly dope, the proper box of flies, and then put it on. It was nearly eight now, and I strung line through the guides of my Orvis quickly as I walked downstream, following the ridge of the stream, looking out over the water.

By the time I stepped into the river, far downstream, a few flies had begun to come off the surface. I saw the waxwings working—dipping and gliding, turning with rapid wing-flaps to catch a mayfly—and then, against the pale blue-dun sky, I saw the flies. There was a cloud of them within a few moments. My hands shook slightly as I dipped them into the water to catch a floating fly. Cream Cahills. Number 12. They were large and lush, and it was a major hatch.

Before I could tie on my fly, I heard a huge splash upstream. A large trout had not taken the fly on the surface but had chased a nymph and then leaped to catch the mayfly when it hatched. There were a few splash rises off to the left, and then I saw the neat sucking down of the water some forty feet directly upstream that meant a fish was taking right on the surface. Then there were rises far upstream, and several off to the right, and then a small sipping rise not ten feet to the right.

My fly was on now, but I stood stock-still and watched the water before casting. There were eight, ten fish feeding regularly. They had taken up fixed feeding positions a few inches beneath the surface, and I could see their fins undulating slowly. They were settling in for a long hard feed.

Finally I began to work out my line, and cast short to a fish some twenty-five feet directly upstream. Ignorantly I hadn't thought to straighten my leader; it lay in loops on the surface. I drew the line back slowly, took out a small patch of rubber, and then worked it up and down the leader, straightening the curls. When I was satisfied with it, I ran the leader through my mouth and then cast again. This time my fly fell a foot above the last ring.

The fish took the fly in a slow gulp, and then fought doggedly. It was a good brown and I was happy to take and release it.

I fished until after dark, taking five solid browns and a small rainbow, and then I headed upstream to a spot where I knew I could get out of the river.

It had been an enormously satisfying evening. The fish had come just fast enough and I had lost myself, and my city worries, in the pleasant task of luring them to the fly. The evening had provided what I'd come to expect of fishing—not barrels of trout but refreshment of my spirit.

It was ten o'clock when I finally got my gear stowed in the car. I could hear voices from down through the dark woods near the river. Sam was cursing wildly, and Jed, the young man, was saying something about a four-pounder—caught or lost, I didn't then know. I'd have liked to go down there where they were, but I was tired and Jane would be waiting. "I'll stay here the whole damned night if I have to!" a voice said. It was Jed's.

As I drove back to the motel, I realized that it did not all have to be so compulsive an affair as I'd often let it become. The desperate search for the perfect rod and the infallible fly; the endless debunking of some new theory; the mania to own more and more equipment, to refine your technique, to be at precisely the right river at the right time—it all didn't matter nearly as much as I'd thought. In fact, that very compulsiveness had torn me not only from my wife and family but from the quiet pursuit of a pastime that should teach all that is counter to compulsiveness.

And that is best practiced with patience, slow patience.

How many times had I fished with a curled leader because some raging fever kept me from the simple gesture of taking a moment, slowing down, taking out a small piece of rubber, and straightening it?

How many moments had I ruined—for myself as well as for my wife—by insane haste?

Those maniacs can stay on the river all night, I thought, *and catch every four-pounder in the whole Middle Branch.* Night fishing was the ultimate compulsion: the big fish compulsion. I'd be more comfortable at the motel than on that cold river—and much safer.

I braked the car beside Lord's in the driveway of the Cloverleaf. It had begun to rain, and I was anxious to get inside. Jane wasn't a monster, whose sole design it was to keep me off the river. She wasn't mean: she simply couldn't understand. And it was perfectly *sane* that she not understand. *I* was mean. My thighs and arms ached from wading and casting, and I thought again of the three men down by the river. Would they fish straight through *in the rain?*

Just then I saw someone sitting alone on a large upturned oak log. What would someone be out in the rain like that for?

It was a woman, and she had her face in her hands. Good grief, it wasn't Jane? No. It couldn't be. What had I possibly done?

The woman was crying bitterly, and I could see paroxysms shake her body.

I left the door of the car open and took several quick steps toward the woman. Then I stopped and my chest collapsed with relief. It wasn't Jane. It was the young woman—Jed's wife, Sam's daughter.

I walked over to her and asked quietly: "Is there anything I can do?"

She didn't move.

"Can I be of any help?" I asked, somewhat louder.

She turned suddenly then and looked at me for a full half minute before speaking. "No, I'm all right," she said, wiping her eyes.

She was really quite beautiful, perhaps twenty-two or twenty-three, with brown hair and delicate features. "Are you hurt?" I asked. "Has something happened to you?" The rain came harder now and her hair was wet and stringy. She had been crying for a long time.

She wrinkled her face into a forced smile, sniffled, wiped her eyes, and said: "I'll be fine in a minute." She looked away. When she turned back and saw me still standing there, she added: "Please go away. I'm fine. I just don't want to talk to anybody."

"Well," I said, "I'll just get my waders in the car and take out my equipment. If there's anything I can . . ."

"Are you a *fish-er-man*, too?" she asked sardonically.

"A fanatic," I said, smiling.

Her eyes grew small and hard. 'Well, I don't want to see any more fishing fanatics tonight, thank you. I've had quite enough of them. For tonight. Forever. You're awful. All of you. You don't know anything else exists. Not anything or anyone. You think fish and dream fish all the time. But *all* the time."

She was beginning to work herself into a real fit now; I wanted to tell her that I *used* to be that kind of fanatic, but that I'd recently begun to be cured. But she never paused. This was a new breed of woman, a champion of causes once lost. Her words poured from her torrentially now, as she called my noble pastime a "mindless, brutish, chauvinist sport, the final infirmity of stupid and childish men."

What could have happened to cause this?

"I don't *want* to be the premier fishing widow of the Western world, thank you. I hate being an Ahab's wife.

I felt embarrassed, awkward. I shrugged my shoulders and wondered why she was telling *me* all this? It was raining hard now and I was anxious to get my gear together and go inside.

"Fanatics? You're *monsters*—all of you. Every one of you men—Sam, his friend, that nut Lord, Jed, and *you*. I've been watching and listening to all of you. You're *too* much."

"I don't understand," I mumbled, apologetically.

"Jed. Do you know my husband? Do you know that crazy fool?"

I nodded.

"Oh, what the hell's the difference? Go on, get your waders and your Payne rods and all your Quill Gordons and variants and Blitzes. I don't care. I don't care at all."

The woman was looking at me with fierce red eyes now; I had ceased being the recently reformed Jack Brooks and had become a symbol of all the fanatics who had plagued all the fishing widows from time immemorial. I couldn't move. I stood there in the rain, dripping, looking intently at her.

"Get the hell away from me!" she shouted.

Still I didn't move. She was a new breed of wife—militant, independent, fiercely covetous of her rights.

When she rose from the oak stump and began coming after me, I don't know if she even knew she had that thick stick in her hand. But I saw it, and it was a big stick, and as she advanced on me, I began backing off, pedaling backward.

"Coward!" she taunted. "Mean, bullying coward!"

"Look, I've done nothing to you," I said, putting my hand up to ward off a possible sudden blow with that stick. "I only wanted to help."

"You're all the same. Every one of you," she shouted. Her eyes were ablaze now, and she kept coming closer, the stick quivering up and down in her hand.

"For God's sake, lady!" I said. "What's the matter with you? Get a hold of yourself and . . ."

And then I felt my foot slide across a moss-slippery rock, I lost my balance, and, falling quickly, felt dull hard stone smash against my head as all went black.

Five

"Does it still hurt, dear?" Jane asked me at breakfast the next morning, half-smiling.

"Yes," I said gruffly, putting a hand on the absurd lump protruding from my scalp, "it still hurts. Little you care."

We were seated at the long cherrywood table, and for some reason my eyes were fixed on a nearby plate. There was a small shiny object on it.

"I knew fishing was a dangerous sport," Jane said. "But you really should try to be more careful."

"That woman is a menace."

"Maybe she's got something against fishermen, dear."

We were alone for a few more minutes; then Betty Warren came in, dressed in neat slacks and a checkered shirt, a simple bandana holding back her hair. Lord came in a few moments later, said hello pleasantly enough, and then sat down next to Betty at the other end of the table. He began chattering away immediately, a bit more deferentially than I'd seen him ever before.

The two older women came in next, without their husbands, and sat at Lord's end of the table. They had on bright summery dresses and spoke with enthusiasm about some plans to go shopping.

The waitress brought our plates of bacon and eggs and I began to eat mine immediately. Beneath the bacon, I noticed I had a bright brook trout monographed on my dish. "Would you please get the salt for me?" Jane asked.

I got up, took a few steps down the line, and looked at the object on the plate closely. It was where the young couple sat— to be exact, on his plate. Right in the middle of it—over the head of a rising cutthroat trout. I looked at it for a moment, breathed deeply, got the salt, and returned to my place beside Jane.

"What is it, dear?" she asked.

"Nothing."

"What was it you were looking at?"

I hesitated. "Look," I said.

She raised herself slightly from her chair, peered over, and said, "Good grief. It's a wedding ring!"

"His or hers?"

"*Hers,* stupid!"

"What's it doing there?"

"What do you *think* it's doing there?"

All three men came in at once, talking all at once—the two older ones and Jed. "I'll get him tonight," said Jed. "I'll switch to one X."

"Never raise him on one X."

"You could raise him on a clothesline after dark," said Sam.

"I'll stick with one X. And a number ten Cahill. Right by that log. I'll bet anything he doesn't move from that spot."

"He won't move."

They sat beside the two wives, at the opposite end of the table from where Jed usually sat.

"He's not going to see it," I whispered to Jane.

"Doesn't look that way—but he'll find out. Sooner or later."

"Where's his wife, the one who was going to maim me?"

"Probably still crying her eyes out. That brute!"

"She's a menace."

"That coarse, miserable fool!"

"You're worse than she is. And he's not such a bad guy," I said. "I was talking to him a couple days ago about that early-morning *Caenis* fishing they've been doing along with the night fishing. He's extremely knowledgeable . . ."

"Poof!"

"And he's crazy about her. She's Sam's daughter, you know —and that guy's one of the best fly-tiers in the East. He must have taught his daughter, because she ties all Jed's flies."

"How perfectly sweet!"

"He told me, 'She ties the best number twenty-four Blue Spinner you ever saw!'"

"Well, he'll just have to tie his own Blue Spinners from now on, won't he dear?"

One of the older women, Sam's wife, came around the table then, and asked Jane if she'd like to spend the day with the other ladies; they were planning to go antiquing and then have lunch together. She said her name was Fanny.

Jane hesitated.

"Go ahead," I said. The woman looked down at Jed's plate and put her hand over her mouth.

"I'd be glad to go," Jane said.

For a moment the woman didn't answer.

Jane said, "When are you leaving?"

Fanny reached out toward the plate and then drew back her hand.

Jane got up, put her hand on the woman's shoulder in a genuinely kind and womanly manner, and said, "What time shall I meet you, Fanny?"

"Oh. Oh, we're . . . leaving right after breakfast." She turned from the plate and smiled at Jane wanly. "Meet us in the lobby . . . right after . . . breakfast."

When she got back to her end of the table, the woman looked at Jed, then across at the plate. She sat stiff as an Egyptian statue.

"You sure you won't mind spending the day with those women?" I asked.

"I'm looking forward to it now," said Jane. "This place is beginning to intrigue me."

"But where's the one who practically killed me? Is she going, too?"

"As I think of it, she's probably a hundred miles from here by now."

"Do you know something?"

"A small matter of woman's intuition. Which doesn't tell you when the Creamhills are biting or matching or whatever they do, but which is good on minor issues like this. Why it's all as plain as the expectation on poor little Jed's face. Listen to him: 'I doubt if he'll come to a nymph, but I'm sure he'll take a Cahill again, if there's a hatch . . .' " She mimicked his words and enthusiasm in a whisper.

A few moments later, we got up and went into the lobby, where we sat together on the couch and leafed through some magazines. Betty Warren and Lord came out first; when she excused herself, he came over to where Jane and I sat and asked if I'd like to fish with him that morning. I told him Jane would be away for the entire day, that we could go out in the afternoon too. He gave me a knowing smile, imagining, I think, that I had taken his advice.

Then the two older women came out, one chattering pleasantly, Fanny ghostly pale and silent.

The two men were just coming to the door, talking raucously about fishing the Cemetery Run that morning, when Jed rushed past them and into the lobby.

One of his hands was balled in a fist, as if he was holding something for dear life.

Everyone stopped talking; everyone froze in their positions and stared at him.

His eyes were wild and hot, and a powerful tension was working in his face and arms. He looked around like a trapped bear, then raced to the manager's office.

We all looked at each other and said nothing. "Sooner," whispered Jane.

He came out in a moment and, without saying a word to anyone, ran to the door, knocking over a lamp that he didn't pause to pick up.

I sighed sadly and told Jane I was going to the room to get my equipment. I heard a car start up loudly, the tires churn up gravel, and saw Jed—hunched over the wheel—race out the driveway.

"Don't be late, dear," Jane called after me sweetly. When I turned, I saw her smiling at me. With the fingers of her right hand, she was sliding, on and off, her wedding band.

Six

When you fish with a man you reveal yourself to him and he to you in a thousand intimate ways. I haven't the slightest notion how I appeared to Lord, other than that he surely recognized a similar disease in me. But he may not have noticed or thought about the matter much: he was a devout angler with immense concentration.

Even though I'd never seen him catch a fish.

That morning I began to watch him more closely. Technically, he was an able if not a brilliant fisherman. His approach was sensible and his presentation more than adequate. He *looked* like a man who would catch fish aplenty. But when we'd fished before, he'd caught nothing.

Still, he was painfully honest and I never heard him complain. He seemed that rare bird who really *does* enjoy himself when not catching fish, and he had displayed none of that vulgar desire to impress companions with tall tales. I knew a fisherman who would miss a fish and call out: "Lost a fifteen-incher"; and others who are forever "driving home the steel," "losing a horse after three incredible leaps," or taking "twenty sizable fish and releasing them"—which I had reason to doubt. Lord made no such claims. A number of times I'd seen his rod whip up, arch for a second, and then snap straight; but during a trip back he'd never once mention having lost a fish.

It may be that, until that morning, he rarely caught them. Perhaps some flaw I could not detect—drag, slow strikes, quick strikes—had prevented him from scoring. But since I'd met him, I'd found the man a rich lode of delightful anecdotes, an endless stream of which, interspersed with theory and angling philosophy and advice, poured from his lips. When I later learned quite how busy and successful an executive he was, I assumed that fishing was the one coherent discipline that enabled him to keep his sanity. Brooding over fly patterns and leader mikes, brooding on the identification of a hatch and the laws of a particular stretch of river, was a sweet and private pleasure that redeemed him from the onus of high finance: his mistress, his "pistol and ball," his Shangri-La. At any rate, the actual taking of a trout had seemed so little of a common occurrence with him that I had assumed it ranked as a feeble excuse for all the rest.

That morning was different.

He took me directly to a new pool, shoved me a boxful of flies I'd never seen before, and said to use them at eleven fifteen, when the hatch started.

"What hatch?" I asked.

"You'll see. Eleven fifteen. For less than an hour."

Then he headed rapidly upstream and told me to meet him at the car, about one o'clock.

The effect of his improbable behavior, this curious change in attitude, had no sooner given way to the sweet, timeless, and rhythmic flicking of my fly than a heavy hatch of a large tan fly I didn't recognize began coming off the water. I watched the flies come off for several minutes, then clipped off my Cahill and began rummaging through my innumerable fly boxes for a suitable imitation. With my new resolve to be patient and thoughtful at such moments, I succeeded in losing no more than the cap to my dry-fly spray and nearly my rod, which I caught as it slipped from my miserably shaking left arm.

The hatch was huge—and the fish were taking.

I was about to tie on a number twelve Hendrickson when I remembered the flies Lord had given me. I also remembered to look at my watch. Eleven twenty-eight.

The flies Lord had given me worked beautifully. I took seven fine browns in less than an hour; watching Lord, upstream, I had seen him take at least a dozen good fish.

"Fabulous, eh?" he said, coming over at a lamb's trot.

"Unbelievable," I said.

"Wait until you see what we get into tonight!"

"Better than this?"

"You'll see."

And I did.

We were with Betty Warren, whom we'd picked up after lunch, and Lord, without asking me where I'd like to go, had taken me to still another new pool, this one down a long, winding dirt road.

We'd suited up about six o'clock, Lord had said there would be nothing until seven thirty, and then we'd all walked slowly across a meadow to the river. Betty, at Lord's adamant insistence, had put on waders this time and taken along her rod and vest. She remained stately, even beautiful, in all the ritualistic trouting grab, but there was something odd about the figure she cut. Perhaps it was only that the vest and waders looked too new.

We drank coffee and talked pleasantly for a half hour, and then the first flies began to come off. Within minutes the sky was clouded with them—huge mayflies, larger than Green Drakes.

In another moment, I saw the first rise.

Only it wasn't a rise; it was as if someone had thrown a watermelon into the water. The huge mayflies brought out the most savage impulses in the trout, and they would charge them with vicious power.

My heart whacked against my chest. I'd never seen such a sight. "Go on, gentlemen," said Betty calmly. "After them."

"Betty," said Lord, "you've been too kind to us both. We *insist* you fish for them first this time. We know how much you enjoy fishing, and we'll have no more of this self-sacrificing."

She protested—not once, but half-a-dozen times. But Lord would hear none of it. All the while they debated the subject, I kept watching—and hearing—the river. It was a symphony—with drums and cymbals now. Twice I wanted to tell him he really shouldn't persuade her, if she really didn't want to fish, but he was using his executive voice now, and at last she relented.

I consoled myself that she'd probably had fifty evenings like this before, caught her fill of such savage trout—that after she'd caught one or two, to satisfy Lord's good grace, her own good grace would lead her to insist that we fish. She was too much a lady.

I watched carefully as she put the round toe-end of her waders into the river, like a child testing the ocean or a lake. *She's a cautious angler,* I thought, knowing I'd have barrel-assed into the center of the stream without delay. This was going to be a memorable sight: she *had* to be a master.

When, after five full minutes of careful hoofing, she had gotten out about fifteen feet, she turned back to us and smiled. "Sure one of you two wouldn't like to try it first?" she whispered loudly.

"Ladies first," Lord whispered back; I watched those watermelon splashes up and down the long run.

"Well," she said. "All right. If you insist. If you really don't want to catch any of these fish . . ."

I saw her bend slightly and search the stream bed with her eyes. *Looking for nymphs,* I thought. *Maybe she'll switch over from dries. God, she's deliberate. A master.*

She took a shuffling step to the right, pulled some line off the reel, waved her fly rod rapidly a few times, and then fell sideways, with a loud screech, flat into the river.

"My God!" shouted Lord, leaping in after her and splashing about like an aging Galahad to where she struggled, half out of the water.

"Oh, God, no!" I muttered as I watched the last of those

monstrous splashes, and the surface of the stream grow placid and still except for those locustlike mayflies still coming off in clouds.

Seven

About noon the next day, Jane and I headed off to explore a dingy old red barn of an antique shop she'd discovered. All the way I kept muttering about that rise, those trout; she smiled and laughed—not hostilely—but said nothing. When I realized I was sounding like a maniac again, I shut my mouth. At the barn we both found several good buys: a silver comb, a couple of old books, two hand-tinted nineteenth-century prints of flies, and a large old porcelain hand-washing bowl that Jane thought would make an excellent planter.

Jane was more talkative once we got the bowl into the car; it was the most expensive item we bought, and I'd been reluctant to part with so much money. Soon she even encouraged me to pass a few fishing remarks, which I did, tentatively.

A couple of miles down the road she mentioned casually that she'd found the two elderly fishing widows extremely sympathetic: they adored their husbands—and absolutely despised fishing. They had made these trips for twenty-five years; they had listened to the endless and meaningless talk about Cahills and *Potamanthus* and this or that so-called run or pool or what-have-you; they had even tried to learn fly casting.

It all bored them silly.

But they had both managed to get their husbands, both fanatics of the first water, deeply in their debt because of the trips. They came from modest daily lives and had found ways to make the trips not only this side of sanity but positively to be loved.

In short, they'd put their husbands on guilt trips—and lived like princesses during these annual jaunts, buying everything they could lay their hands on, and even going on day-long binges. One of them, Jane said, had pulled a bottle of J & B from her big purse the minute they'd left the motel, the other had produced three plastic cups from hers.

Jane said she'd expected to eat at a modest coffee shop but that instead they'd insisted on taking her to the Alexandria, the most expensive restaurant in town—where they'd had three or four more drinks, a lavish lunch, and two hours of spirited, revealing talk. "They positively weaved out of that place," she said, "and then we headed for the shops."

Jane noted that it was two o'clock and asked solicitously whether I didn't want to head back, to get ready for the evening rise. I said I'd just as well shop with her, if she didn't mind.

"Do you mean it?" she asked. 'You *really* want to shop with me?"

"I'm not one of those maniacs. Of course I do."

"You're not going to tell me you've decided to fish all night, like Jed did two nights ago, on their *first* wedding anniversary, or fly up to Canada with Lord and leave me stranded."

"I'd be afraid you'd get drunk and buy out the town.'

She looked at me sternly and then smiled. "Well, I think it's a nice gesture on your part anyway. Even if you are afraid."

"I like shopping," I said.

"You hate it."

"Yup. Hate it."

"Thought so." She frowned. "But as long as you'll take me, and not be a grunting old groucher, I'll tell you a secret. One good turn deserves another."

"What secret?"

"There's a lot of action at the motel."

I turned and looked over at her. "What kind of *action?*"

"You swear you won't tell?"

"Cross my heart."

"Well, Jed and Mary you know about. Except that he found her at the bus station, and they've gone off together. Just like that."

"You mean I won't have to face that wild woman again?"

"No one knows where they've gone. But they went together— and Jed called the motel and told the manager to give his fishing tackle, all of it, to his father-in-law."

"For good?"

"Who knows?"

"I doubt it. You don't kick the habit that easily."

"You can't tell."

"He'd never betray the brotherhood of the . . ."

"Bets?"

I saw the basket shop up ahead and began to slow down. "Want to stop there?" I asked.

"Not today. It looks too crowded. Anyway, I'm enjoying the drive."

We were silent for a few moments, and then I said, "What's there not to tell about all of that?"

"Well, don't talk about it, that's all. But there's more. At a higher level."

"And what's that?"

"Promise you won't tell?"

"Of course not."

"Betty Warren . . ."

"A remarkable woman. One in a million."

Jane smiled, took out a cigarette, lit it slowly, and then said, "You know she's always hated fishing?"

The words were crushing. "I don't believe it." Was there no idyll then, no dream marriage?

"The ladies told me. They've known her for years, since she and her husband first started to come up to the Cloverleaf, twenty years ago. It was a notorious situation."

No idyll. I couldn't speak.

"At first she was absolutely inconsolable. She'd been brought up to like art and music and tennis, and she simply couldn't abide coming up to this mosquito-ridden place where she was left alone for hours at a time. All the rustic clothing, the bad art, the fish talk, the homey wives of the other fishermen . . . it was all too much for her."

"I understand," I said quietly.

"She was like that for years. Fanny and Margaret couldn't get her to loosen up one bit. They tried to be nice—but she snubbed them. She'd just go off by herself and read . . . or cry."

"Sounds awful."

"There was talk of divorce," she said, "and even talk of suicide. It was that serious."

"*Fishing* caused all that?"

"That's the gossip."

"But what changed her? And why is she here now?"

"Nobody's quite sure. Two or three years before he died, she began to go out with him, and everything seemed all right after that. Everyone thought she was doing it just to please him, to keep the marriage together, and there'd been talk of a terminal disease —but then when he died she began coming back by herself. That was the strange part."

"To fish? I thought she couldn't abide it?"

"That's what everyone thought," said Jane.

"Why else would she come back? Not for the trout prints on the lampshades, or to swat mosquitoes. But I'd think she'd want to avoid fish camps like the plague."

"Well . . . you promised you wouldn't tell."

"Tell what, for gosh sakes?"

"She's after a husband."

I was stunned. "Impossible! Why would she want another fish nut? That makes no sense. Why would a woman who had suffered all those years deliberately go back for more punishment? She's obviously been left well off—why doesn't she go back to her tennis and golf and yachts?"

"The ladies don't know. But she came up and took a fly-fishing course—which she *flunked*—"

"You mean she *can't* fish?"

"Not a whit."

"Well, who do the ladies think she's after? Oh, no. Not . . ."

"Yes. Mr. A. C. Lord."

"Impossible. The man who wrote the book on independence and the joys of bachelorhood?"

"That's their theory."

"Lord?"

"That's what they say. And there's evidence for it."

'Well, I don't believe it—but if she *is* fishing for him, it's a lost cause."

"Wouldn't want to make another bet would you?"

"I wouldn't take your money."

"Two bits?"

"All right. All right."

"But you can't say a word. You promised. You can't inter-fere in any way."

"But why would she want him? *Why,* Jane?"

"That," said my wife, drawing deftly upon her meager knowledge of the literature, "will have to remain another minor chalk stream mystery."

Eight

By Sunday of the next week, when we were to leave, a re-markable change had overtaken my friend Allen C. Lord. He was catching scores of trout regularly now, but I could see that his equanimity had been sorely disturbed. He was not himself. He mumbled to himself, he often seemed sadly distracted. I was afraid for his health.

He and Betty Warren were frequent companions, and I queried Jane several times about whether I shouldn't warn the man that he was being fished over with a long line and a delicate leader.

"You promised."

"But it seems cruel and immoral."

"For two older people to find each other, dear? Where's your heart?"

"It's not exactly that way. She's using her dead husband's logbooks for bait. It's ghastly."

"Poof! Lord always seemed like such a lonely old man to me anyway, with nothing to keep him warm at night except fish dreams."

"He seemed perfectly happy—and he was. He never caught any fish, but he enjoyed himself. Immensely. Now he's miser-able."

"Are *you* miserable, dear, just because we're married?"

"That's different. Look, I've *got* to tell him."

"You promised. And that's it."

I fished alone for an hour or two around noon, but my heart wasn't in it. There was no hatch, so I fished a nymph. I caught nothing, and when I came off the water I knew I was packing away my equipment for the rest of the year.

Still, it had been an instructive, even pleasant trip. After those first few days, I'd caught some fish, enjoyed being with Jane, listened to some marvelous stories, and watched a drama of high import unfold before me.

But why was she after him?

She didn't need his money. She *couldn't* want another fisherman. She was attractive, and certainly young enough to catch her fish elsewhere, of a less compulsive breed.

Vengeance?

I didn't want to believe it.

I'd seen one woman strike out, and at me, out of such vengeance, but she was of a different generation, a different time. I couldn't believe that Betty Warren, a woman of such obvious refinement, would take out the pain of a few miserable fishing trips with her late husband on a perfect stranger.

Or was it force of habit? Could she have possibly become, in a sort of masochistic way, addicted to the role of fishing widow? Had she grown to enjoy it, the way those other old fishing widows did?

A *major* chalk stream mystery.

I packed the car slowly and carefully that evening. The sun was already covered by clouds. It would be an overcast evening— cool by seven thirty. *That ought to get them a-stirring,* I thought. I had visions of that watermelon rise—and of Betty Warren falling in.

Sam and his friend whisked by on their way to their car; they paused for a moment, expressed their regrets that we hadn't fished together, said they were going after a four-pounder that began night feeding at ten o'clock—the one Jed had pricked his last night out—and rushed off, jabbering.

Fanny and Margaret hugged Jane warmly, whispered and laughed, and headed off in another car, "to paint the town red,"

Fanny said. I noticed they were pleasantly drunk, and that Margaret had on a new suede jacket. Jane waved to them as if they were old friends.

As I started up the motor, I saw Lord come around the corner of the building, arm in arm with Betty Warren. It was the first time they'd displayed any public intimacy. He looked drawn and worn, perhaps from having caught too many fish. And he was dressed, I noticed, in a tie and jacket: this would be the first evening of fishing he'd missed.

When I waved to him and tooted the horn, he nodded and smiled wanly. But when I leaned out the side window to holler a good-bye, he grew full of determination, like a trout that's suddenly seen the net. He raced to the car, without so much as an excuse to his companion, who stood calmly near the building.

"For God's sake, man," he whispered hoarsely. "Do you *have* to leave?"

"Due back at my desk tomorrow morning."

"Then there's nothing to be done?"

"Nothing," I said.

"I hope you have good fishing," said Jane.

He ignored her. "Look, Jack, will you do me a tremendous favor?"

"If I can."

"Call me tomorrow night."

"What for?"

"Just call. About six o'clock. When we'll be at the table. I'll pretend it's a business call. That's it. Don't mind if I say things you don't understand. That's it. That's what I'll say." He was almost muttering to himself.

"Sure," I said, "I'll call."

"Six o'clock?"

"On the nose."

He could have kissed me he was so happy. "Ought to have them by then," he mumbled. "That ought to be enough time. Right?"

"What are you talking about?" I said.

"Nothing. Absolutely nothing. Nothing for you to concern

yourself about, old man. That's great. You'll call. Fine. You *will* call, won't you? I can depend on you, can't I?''

I nodded, and in a few moments we were on the road, headed away from the Cloverleaf toward the city, away from the gentle rivers for another year.

The next night at six o'clock sharp, I had my hand on the phone. But Jane grabbed it. She frowned and shook her head and insisted I had made a prior promise to her not to interfere, to let this thing take its natural course, for better or worse.

We debated the matter intently for an hour, and I finally walked away, mumbling. In the living room I found a copy of Skues, and flipped the pages for a few moments. But for some reason I couldn't concentrate on it, and finally settled for Jane Austen, which I read until midnight, until Emma Woodhouse found out who she was and became it, and then earned the right to marry Mr. Knightly. Who himself had waited patiently. Yes. *C'est le plus patient qui gagne.*